Learning from the Prayers
of Old Testament Leaders

GENERAL EDITOR

KEN COLEY

LifeWay Press®
Nashville, Tennessee

Production Team

Content Editor
Reid Patton

Team Leader
Joel Polk

Production Editor
David Haney

Manager, Short-Term Discipleship
Brian Daniel

Art Director
Jon Rodda

Director, Discipleship & Groups Ministry
Michael Kelley

ISBN 978-1-5359-0795-8 • Item 005804354

Dewey decimal classification: 248.3
Subject headings: PRAYER / BIBLE. O.T.—HISTORY OF BIBLICAL EVENTS / PRAYERS

To order additional copies of this resource, write to LifeWay Resources Customer Service; One LifeWay Plaza; Nashville, TN 37234; email orderentry@lifeway.com; order online at LifeWay.com; fax 615-251-5933; call toll free 800-458-2772; or visit the LifeWay Christian Store serving you.

Printed in the United States of America

Groups Ministry Publishing • LifeWay Resources • One LifeWay Plaza • Nashville, TN 37234

CONTENTS

ABOUT THE AUTHORS

KEN COLEY (general editor; week 12, "The Prayer of Nehemiah") is a senior professor of Christian education at Southeastern Baptist Theological Seminary in Wake Forest, North Carolina, where he has taught since 1996. He graduated from Wake Forest University with a BA in English and began his teaching career in 1974. Ken completed his master's degree at The College of William and Mary (1979) and his doctor of education at the University of Maryland (1993). He also currently serves as a teaching pastor at Richland Creek Community Church. He frequently speaks at conferences throughout the United States and has made presentations internationally in Canada, Haiti, Cuba, Panama, The Democratic Republic of the Congo, and Ukraine. Ken has been married to his wife, Kathy, for forty-three years, and they have two adult children, Scott and Caitlin. When he isn't writing or teaching, he enjoys playing with his two German shepherds, kayaking, and running 5K events.

MIGUEL ECHEVARRIA (week 1, "The Prayer of Moses") is an assistant professor of New Testament and Greek and the director of Hispanic leadership development at Southeastern Baptist Theological Seminary. Before joining Southeastern, Miguel served as an assistant professor of Christian studies at The University of Mobile. Miguel received his PhD from The Southern Baptist Theological Seminary in Louisville, Kentucky. His publications include *The Future Inheritance of Land in the Pauline Epistles* (Pickwick, 2019) and several essays and articles. He is married to Hollie, and they have three daughters, Miriam, Esther, and Eunice.

CHUCK LAWLESS (week 2, "The Prayer of Joshua") serves as a professor of evangelism and missions, the dean of doctoral studies, and the vice president for spiritual formation at Southeastern Baptist Theological Seminary, in addition to serving as the team leader for theological-education strategists for the International Mission Board. He previously served as the vice president of the International Mission Board, the dean of the Billy Graham School at Southern Seminary, and a local-church pastor in Ohio. The author of several books on spiritual warfare, Chuck is a graduate of The University of the Cumberlands (1985) and The Southern Baptist Theological Seminary (1992, 1997). He and his wife, Pam, live in Wake Forest, North Carolina.

AMY WHITFIELD (week 3, "The Prayer of Deborah") is the director of marketing and communications at Southeastern Baptist Theological Seminary. She graduated from Converse College (1998) with a BA in politics and completed her MA in Christian studies at Southeastern Baptist Theological Seminary (2018). Amy has spent her career in denominational service, working for multiple Southern Baptist entities and serving the Convention in a voluntary capacity for many years. She's also a writer, speaker, and podcast host. She's married to Keith, and they live in Wake Forest with their two children, Mary and Drew. Amy loves great stories.

SHERRY BLANKENSHIP (week 4, "The Prayer of Hannah") is the lead chaplain at Missouri Baptist Medical Center in Saint Louis West County. She also leads RUBIES women's ministry at Parkway Baptist Church, where her husband, Dwight, is the pastor. Triplets Joshua (Erica), Jonathan (Amanda), and Anna Joy in heaven trained them for five grandchildren two and under. Sherry, who earned a BS from The University of Southern Mississippi, an MRE from Southwestern Baptist Theological Seminary, and a DMin from Midwestern Baptist Theological Seminary, is an Association of Professional Chaplains board-certified chaplain. She authored *Draw Near: One Pilgrim's Journey through Grief to the Lap of Jesus*. Her U.S. and international speaking assignments often train church leaders and volunteers for effective ministry to sick and dying people. Sherry loves playing with her grandchildren, collecting old transferware, and leading people to know Jesus.

JOHN EWART (week 5, "The Prayer of Solomon") is the associate vice president for global theological initiatives and ministry centers and an associate professor of missions and pastoral leadership at Southeastern Baptist Theological Seminary. He's the president of A New Normal Church and Denominational Consultation and Conferencing, an author, a conference leader, and a consultant. John graduated from Baylor University, Southwestern Baptist Theological Seminary, and The Southern Baptist Theological Seminary. John served in pastoral ministry for more than twenty years, regularly serves as an interim pastor, has conducted missions, education, and/or consulting projects in more than sixty nations, and has personally participated in more than one dozen church starts. John also serves as the vice president for Mojdeh Ministries, training Persian church leaders globally. He's married to Tresa, and they have three children and two grandchildren.

J. CHRIS SCHOFIELD (week 6, "The Prayer of Joel") is the director of the Office of Prayer for Evangelization and Spiritual Awakening with the Baptist State Convention of North Carolina, where he has served since 2004. Before going to North Carolina, Chris served with the North American Mission Board as the manager of the Prayer Evangelism Unit from 1997 to 2004. He has pastored two churches and occasionally serves as an adjunct professor at Southeastern Baptist Theological Seminary. Chris enjoys writing; teaching; and preaching on the topics of prayer, evangelism, revival, and spiritual awakening. He completed his BA at Gardner-Webb College (1987) and his MDiv (1991), Th.M (1995), and PhD (2001) at Southeastern Baptist Theological Seminary. Chris and his wife, Tamee, have four daughters, two sons-in-law, and five grandchildren. They reside in Wake Forest, North Carolina.

DAVID HORNER (week 7, "The Prayer of Jehoshaphat") planted Providence Baptist Church in Raleigh, North Carolina, in 1978, where he was the senior pastor for more than thirty-seven years. Currently he serves as the executive director of Equipped for Life, a ministry designed to equip Christian leaders. His equipping ministry incorporates preaching and teaching, writing (the author of four books), overseas missions ventures, personal mentoring/coaching, and church consulting. A native of Graham, North Carolina, David received a BA from Wake Forest University, an MDiv from Gordon-Conwell Theological Seminary, and a PhD from Southeastern Baptist Theological Seminary. He and his wife, Cathy, have three sons and five grandchildren.

WILLIAM T. BRANCH (week 8, "The Prayer of Hezekiah") began studies at Philadelphia Biblical University (formerly Philadelphia College of Bible), eventually graduated from Lancaster Bible College, and received his ThM from Dallas Theological Seminary. He went on to coplant and copastor an urban church in north Philadelphia. Duce is also a Christian hip-hop artist who has recorded independently and as a founding member of The Cross Movement. He's married to Michelle, and they have five children.

DAVID SIMS (week 9, "The Prayer of Jonah") serves as the senior pastor of Richland Creek Community Church in Wake Forest, North Carolina. He has been pastoring since 1997. David graduated from the University of Maryland with a BA in economics (1989). He worked for the Marriott Corporation in Washington, D.C., before the Lord called him into full-time ministry. David completed his MDiv (1999) at Southeastern Seminary and is completing his PhD in theology. David has been married to his wife, Emily, for twenty-one years, and they have three children, Grace, Jake, and Maddy. He greatly enjoys doing mission work in countries that need evangelism and discipleship.

ALLAN MOSELEY (week 10, "The Prayer of Habakkuk") is a senior professor of Old Testament and Hebrew at Southeastern Baptist Theological Seminary, where he has taught since 1996. His undergraduate study was at Samford University, and he earned MDiv and PhD degrees at New Orleans Baptist Theological Seminary. Before beginning his teaching career, Moseley served as a pastor, and he continues to serve regularly as an interim pastor. He has also lectured and preached throughout the country and internationally. He has written, edited, or contributed to nine books and has written more than one hundred articles and Bible studies. Allan and his wife, Sharon, have three married children and eight grandchildren. He enjoys spending time with his family, fishing, and reading.

DANNY AKIN (week 11, "The Prayer of Daniel") is the president of Southeastern Baptist Theological Seminary, where he also serves as a professor of preaching and theology. He and his wife, Charlotte, have four sons, all of whom currently serve in the ministry; four daughters-in-law; and twelve grandchildren. Danny and Charlotte have traveled to Sudan, Turkey, the Middle East, Kenya, Asia, Central Asia, Thailand, India, and Paraguay, serving students and missionaries and sharing the gospel.

HOW TO USE THIS STUDY

Welcome to a twelve-week journey through significant prayers of Old Testament leaders. Here's how this Bible study works.

GROUP EXPERIENCE

START. Your group session will most likely begin here with a few questions designed to help you introduce the week's topic of study and encourage everyone to talk. A brief background of the Scripture passage under consideration is also provided.

WATCH. Key statements from the video session are provided so that you can follow along as you listen to the video teaching.

DISCUSS. This section should be the main component of your group time. The questions provided are designed to help facilitate the group study on a selected Old Testament prayer. Your goal during this time is to better understand and apply the teaching of Scripture to your lives.

GROUP PRAYER. Each group session ends with a prayer activity consisting of four prompts designed to facilitate group prayer. The practice of prayer is an essential component of the study, so be sure to allot an adequate amount of time to call out to the Lord in response to Scripture.

PERSONAL EXPERIENCE

PERSONAL STUDY. Each week provides five devotions that will guide members to examine the text of Scripture more deeply. These personal studies should help participants better understand key Old Testament prayers.

PRAYER. In addition to the devotion, each day features a corresponding prayer exercise that uses the same prompts as the group prayers. The goal of this activity is to immerse group members in the practice of daily, meaningful prayer in response to God's Word.

THE PRAY METHOD

All Christians recognize the importance of prayer, yet many would admit to being unsatisfied with their prayer lives. We've all been there. You start to pray, but then your mind wanders, and before you know it, you've lost focus and can't remember what you're praying about. Using a system for praying can help you focus as you pray and can give you a repeatable pattern to use as you talk with the Lord.

Each group session and personal study relies on the acronym PRAY, a method of prayer that employs common features found in biblical prayers. As this study will demonstrate, the Bible is filled with the prayers of the saints, and we can learn to pray by following the examples in Scripture. PRAY stands for the following components of prayer.

PRAISE

While much our prayer life involves making our requests to God, prayers in the Bible almost always start by praising God for who He is. Worship shouldn't be confined to the musical portion of a Sunday service. It should define our lives and our prayers as well.

REPENT

Recognizing who God is leads us to recognize who we aren't. Seeing God clearly always moves God's people to repentance. Confessing our sins and receiving God's forgiveness and grace builds fellowship with God and renews our spirit as our will is aligned with His will.

APPLY

When we're confronted with biblical truth, we should always seek to apply it. Application happens in prayer as we ask God to make His will effective in our lives in partnership with the Holy Spirit.

YIELD

Biblical revelation calls for a biblical response. The goal of prayer is to yield our lives to God's directions and embrace His direction for our lives.

TIPS FOR LEADING A SMALL GROUP

PRAYERFULLY PREPARE. Pray for each group session beforehand. Ask the Holy Spirit to work through you and the group discussion as you point to Jesus each week through God's Word.

A good small-group experience has the following characteristics.

EVERYONE PARTICIPATES. Encourage everyone to ask questions, share responses, or read aloud.

NO ONE DOMINATES. Be sure your time speaking as a leader takes up less than half your time together as a group. Politely guide discussion if anyone dominates.

DON'T RUSH. Don't feel that a moment of silence is a bad thing. People often need time to think about their responses to questions they've just heard or to gain courage to share what God is stirring in their hearts.

AFFIRM AND FOLLOW UP ON INPUT. Make sure you point out something true or helpful in a response. Don't just move on. Build community with follow-up questions, asking how other people have experienced similar things or how a truth has shaped their understanding of God and the Scripture you're studying.

KEEP GOD'S WORD CENTRAL. Opinions and experiences can be helpful, but God has given us the truth. Trust Scripture to be the authority and God's Spirit to work in people's lives. You can't change anyone, but God can. Continually point people to the Word and to active steps of faith.

KEEP CONNECTING. Encourage group members with thoughts, commitments, or questions from the session by connecting through emails, texts, and social media. Build deeper friendships by planning or spontaneously inviting group members to join you outside your regularly scheduled group time for meals; fun activities; and projects around your home, church, or community. The more people are comfortable with one another and involved in one another's lives, the more they'll look forward to being together.

DEDICATION

If you hadn't known Bill was sick with a serious disease, you probably wouldn't have realized the preacher that morning was suffering with cancer that would slowly take his life. He had shared with me earlier in the week that he felt normal the fourth week of each month, during which he had no chemotherapy treatments. He had scheduled me to preach that morning in December 2017, but he called and asked me to step aside and allow him to return to his pulpit. God had inspired him with a message, and he felt like preaching for the first time in recent weeks.

Bill remarked in that conversation, without complaint or rancor, "Most days following chemo treatments, I have enough energy to get out of bed and walk to the family room, where I collapse into my overstuffed recliner. And I sit there all day until bedtime. But this week I feel that I can preach. I hope you don't mind."

No one knew—not even Bill—that this would be his last message.

Dr. Bill Bowyer stood straight and tall, shoulders square, and spoke with a strong voice to the congregation of Wake Cross Roads Baptist Church, as if nothing were holding him back, as he had done almost every Sunday for two decades. "You might think it odd," he began, "that I've selected for my text during this Christmas season Jonah 2, in which we read Jonah's prayer while inside a large fish." And so he opened what I thought at the time to be the best message I had ever heard my friend preach.

As I listened, drawn into the reluctant prophet's predicament and impassioned prayer, the Holy Spirit jolted me with an idea. This message needed to be communicated beyond the walls of this congregation and community. The truth from this passage must be broadcast to a larger audience. Less than ten minutes into his message, the outline for a Bible study was implanted in my heart. Bill and his lovely wife, Deana, had invited Kathy and me to lunch that day, and over lunch I jotted down a working title and an outline on a napkin. I explained to Bill that the Holy Spirit had inspired me as he preached that morning, and I pitched the possibility that the two of us could collaborate on a Bible study.

We parted that day with a shared commitment to develop the study you hold in your hands. I prayed that this project would provide my friend with a tangible task to focus on during the grueling surgery and recovery ahead. Unfortunately, the cancer would claim his life in early spring before he finished. This study is dedicated to the memory of Dr. Bill Bowyer.

INTRODUCTION

"Are we lost?" my wife asks me as I pull to a stop at an unfamiliar intersection.

"I think we're good," I confidently respond as I stare at the crossroads in front of me.

We've been here before. What happens next is predictable. She suggests one path based solely on the advice presented by her GPS. She trusts the soft voice coming through the car speakers without reservation. I, on the other hand, am an explorer who relies on his gut to determine his next move. My sense of direction has proved dependable in the past, and I'm committed to my instincts and prior experiences. We'll wait and see how this works out.

On a frigid night in December many years ago we were frozen at a much different crossroads. Earlier that day we had laid our second child, a stillborn little boy, to rest in a snowy grave. Painful questions filled our minds. Why had this happened? Was this someone's fault? Would we have enough courage to try again? Answers were nowhere in sight. There was no GPS, and my instincts were paralyzed. As believers in Christ, we clung to each other and to our Savior and prayed.

Our prayers reveal much about our inner life. What aches and pains are we experiencing? What are our greatest joys and deepest sorrows? What major decisions need to be made before we can move forward? The content of our prayers tells us about the influence of success and failure in our lives and the impact of danger or insecurity. Prayers also allow us the opportunity to peer into the well of our deepest convictions. What do we celebrate about who God is, and to what extent are we willing to trust our Creator?

So it is with the moving prayers recorded in Scripture from the hearts of God's servants in the Old Testament. The authors of this study invite you to walk the paths of some of the amazing men and women the Lord used in His plan for humankind in preparation for the coming Messiah. As you study these Old Testament passages, we hope you'll do the following.

1. Deeply consider how each prayer connects to your ministry and your personal challenges. Make mental notes about each prayer for future applications. Perhaps God will use this study in special ways to prepare you for His glory through upcoming events in your life.

2. Elaborate your understanding as you read and meditate. That is, put the truth from God's Word into your own words, being careful to maintain the precise meaning of the passage and prayer. As you express biblical truth in your own words, it becomes part of who you are and your everyday communication.

3. Discover the patterns of adoration and supplication that are unique to each prayer. As you learn from these powerful prayers, you can speak to God from fresh perspectives and meditate on His glory in new ways.
4. Expect the Holy Spirit to work in and through your prayer life to change you and strengthen your walk of discipleship. How does He want you to change not only the substance of your prayers but also the thoughts and actions of your daily life?
5. Look for leadership insights from each prayer and ask the Lord to strengthen your perspectives and skills for future ministry. Following some prayers in this study, the leaders moved boldly; following some, the leaders rejoiced greatly; and after some, they simply watched patiently as God acted mightily.
6. Assess the strengths and weaknesses of your church family in light of the context of each prayer. How might the Lord bring about revival and renewal in your congregation as a result of this study?

Questions related to these six challenges appear in each week's study. We hope you'll respond to these interludes in each day's study by reflecting on new ideas, recording your plans for change, and discussing points of application with other group members. In addition, we wanted to review with our readers the way each leader and each prayer blends into the larger historical narrative of the Old Testament. We hope these snapshots will increase your understanding of each scene in God's drama.

Are you lost? Perhaps you can benefit from the training U.S. Marines receive in preparation for marching through uncharted forests or jungle terrain. Marines are taught to find high ground or climb a tree in order to visualize a fixed spot in the direction of their destination. Using a compass, the marine takes a compass reading (his azimuth) that corresponds to the specific point he should travel. Once he's back on the trail, that compass heading helps him arrive at his desired destination, despite the fact that he couldn't see it during his journey.

Isn't prayer a lot like shooting an azimuth? Throughout each day, when we're uncertain about where we're headed, we talk to the Lord and read Scripture to get our bearings and make sure we're on the right path. We believe the Lord will use this study in your life to provide guidance for your spiritual journey.

WEEK 1

The Prayer of Moses

START

Welcome to group session 1 of *Praying at the Crossroads*.

Use the following questions to begin the session.

Have you ever wondered why people live in sin for decades or why people suffer for prolonged periods of time?

Does suffering make you doubt God's goodness? Does it make you wonder when God will act on behalf of the righteous?

In what circumstances have you asked questions like the previous ones?

Few people would deny that we live in a sinful world. You're not alone in asking some of the foregoing questions.

Moses also had such thoughts. God had used him to deliver a generation of Israelites from slavery in Egypt and through the wilderness until they were at the point of inheriting the promised land. Despite being witnesses to God's salvation, the wilderness generation struggled with sin and rebellion. They tested God and grumbled in spite of His goodness. They practiced sexual immorality and worshiped false idols. Seeing their sin, God was angry. Their acts were so detestable that He promised that the whole generation would die in the wilderness, never reaching their destination, never entering the land (see Num. 14:23; 26:65). Facing the prospect of death, Moses wrote the psalm we know today as Psalm 90, which acknowledged God's anger and prayed for mercy and restoration.[1] Though the first generation would perish, Moses prayed that the covenant God would permit his future offspring to see better days.

These events are no less relevant for Christians today. Paul said the wilderness tradition was recorded "for our instruction, on whom the ends of the ages have come" (1 Cor. 10:11). We too are in a sinful wilderness, for we live in an age characterized by sin, oppression, and rebellion against God. Our hope, like that of Moses, is that God will deliver us to a place of permanent flourishing.

Use these statements to follow along as you watch video session 1.

God is the eternal Creator God.

God is eternal, yet man is mortal.

Moses confessed that the Israelites had sinned against the eternal God of the universe.

Moses prayed for deliverance that comes about only by crying out to the covenant faithfulness of God.

When Moses looked at the land of blessing, he saw beyond that land to a better land that was to come.

Moses prayed for blessing, a time of flourishing for God's people.

We, like the Israelites, are also in a wilderness.

Because of faith in Christ, we have the same hope Moses had: that we will be those successive generations that will experience long life in a new creation, in a better land of blessing that's promised to God's people.

Application from Moses' Prayer

1. The same God who created us will one day deliver us.

2. We should examine ourselves as we suffer and wait.

3. Encourage others.

4. Know that we are not alone; God is with us.

Video sessions available at lifeway.com/prayingatthecrossroads or with a subscription to smallgroup.com

DISCUSS

Use the following questions to discuss the video teaching.

Read Psalm 90.

How long had the Israelites suffered under God's wrath? How might they have felt while living under prolonged judgment?

What did Moses request God to do on behalf of His people?

In Psalm 90 Moses wrote a prayer to God while suffering in the wilderness. The Israelites had sinned against the Creator God, making Him angry and bringing His wrath on themselves. Acknowledging the brevity of human life, Moses prayed that God would deliver His people from distress. His hope, however, wasn't for salvation into a spiritual realm of bliss. In view of the biblical story line, he anticipated that God would deliver His people from the wilderness into a land of flourishing, a land that has now been expanded to include the entire re-created cosmos over which the Messiah will reign (see Ps. 2; Isa. 65–66; Dan. 7–8; Rev. 21–22).

Why should you pray, like Moses, that God will save you from your present suffering and difficulties?

Based on Moses' prayer, what confidence should you have in asking God to deliver you into a renewed world where suffering will no longer exist?

As someone who hoped in God, Moses was a child of Abraham. In Galatians 3 Paul tells us that people who have faith in Christ are also sons and daughters of Abraham and heirs of the promises. Thus, because we have the same hope as Moses, let's fix our eyes on the blessed Savior who will deliver us from the present world of sin and lead us into an eternal place of blessing. Until then we're to persevere in our faith, enduring trials, difficulties, and suffering at the hands of the unrighteous, knowing that Jesus will return to deliver us and renew His good creation. We long for this. We persevere for this.

Why should our prayers include hope for the day when we'll be in a place where we'll experience peace and comfort in the presence of Christ, our King?

God saw Israel's suffering, and He sees yours too. Whatever you're going through, God sees your pain. He sees your trials. Night won't last forever. Morning will come soon—and permanently.

How should we pray when we don't feel that God sees our pain and hardship?

One struggle this side of heaven is the one that comes from extended suffering we feel God isn't addressing. It's one thing to know God sees our suffering; it's another to believe He will do something about it. In those moments, like Moses, let's fix our eyes on what's to come, knowing that soon all will be as it should be. When Jesus returns, we'll no longer hurt, no longer mourn, no longer suffer under oppression. Instead, His people will be blessed all of their days. This is the lasting state for which Isaiah longed when he wrote:

> Those who trust in the LORD
> will renew their strength;
> they will soar on wings like eagles;
> they will run and not become weary,
> they will walk and not faint.
> ISAIAH 40:31

Just hold on a bit longer. Your God will soon make all things right.

How does fixing our eyes on our future hope help us grasp that our trials are temporary?

Why is it important for us to realize that a renewed world of blessing awaits us that won't be corrupted by the curse of sin, pain, and death?

GROUP PRAYER

Use the following PRAY framework to pray together as a group.

In light of what we've studied today, pray together as a group, using the following prompts to guide your experience together. You'll repeat this exercise at the end of each day's personal study. Use the biblical prayer we studied to guide your own. Read each prompt aloud and encourage group members to lift up prayers based on these prompts silently or aloud, depending on their comfort level.

PRAISE *God for who He is and what He has done.*
God is the Creator and Sustainer of the universe, the One who sustained Israel in the wilderness. Praise Him for sustaining you in the present age.

REPENT *of unconfessed sins and accept Christ's forgiveness.*
Israel egregiously sinned in the wilderness, bringing God's wrath on themselves. We must recognize that we too have sinned against God. Repent of any sin and look to Jesus, God's Son, for forgiveness.

APPLY *the truths you've learned by committing to action.*
Moses prayed for God to have mercy on His people. Perhaps you're reaping the results of unrepented sin, even secret sin (see Ps. 90:8). Commit to repent of sin and look to the cross for forgiveness. The blood of God's Son is sufficient to make your sins "as white as snow" (Isa. 1:18).

YIELD *your life to God's will and kind providence.*
Moses not only dealt with his personal sin but also confronted others with their sin. In Exodus 32, for example, he confronted Aaron for his role in enabling the children of Israel to worship a golden calf. If a Christian in your life, such as a friend, family member, or church member, is living in open, unrepented sin, prayerfully consider confronting them, knowing a little pain now may lead to their repentance and restoration (see Matt. 18; 1 Cor. 5).

Close by praying for specific requests that arose during the session.

CONFIDENCE IN THE ETERNAL GOD

> **Read Psalm 90:1-2.**

Moses began the psalm by asserting that God had been the "refuge" of every Israelite (v. 1). In other words, God had been the nation's source of protection and safety from their enemies (see Deut. 33:27; Ps. 71:3).[2] Though true for every generation, the assurance of God's care would have been especially meaningful to the Israelites as they wandered in the desert. With no land of their own, no fortress or place to hide, Moses' words would have sounded a note of hope amid suffering.

Moses' hope for refuge was in the eternal God (see Ps. 90:2). No one created God. No one gave Him shape. No one gave Him life. God created the world—humans, plants, animals, stars, absolutely everything. We find this truth succinctly summarized in Genesis 1:1: "In the beginning God created the heavens and the earth."

In view of His eternality, it's incredible that God chose to be Israel's refuge. He delivered His people from slavery in Egypt and was now leading them through the wilderness. The Israelites should have had no doubts about God's goodness and no fears about their future. Their trust should have been in the Lord, for He had promised to guide them to the land sworn to Abraham and his descendants (see Gen. 12; 15; 17).

Our hope, like that of the Israelites, is in the eternal God. Though we're sojourners, God sent Jesus Christ to deliver us from the present sinful age (see Gal. 4:4). He created us, and He will restore us to a place of rest (see Rev. 21–22). No matter what hardship we struggle with, no matter how desperate circumstances seem, we should never lose hope. Our God made us, and He will see to it that we arrive at our eternal dwelling place.

PRAYER

Enter this time with your Bible and your heart open.
Based on the truths of Scripture, answer the following
questions and let them lead you to a time of prayer.

PRAISE

God saves people who've trusted in Jesus' death and resurrection in their place for their sins. If you've placed your confidence in Christ, are you praising God for delivering you from sin? Are you praising Him for promising to bring you into an eternal place of blessing?

REPENT

Israel had seen God's saving hand but still doubted His goodness. When do you also doubt God's goodness? Do you trust that your future is in the hands of the Creator God?

APPLY

How intentional are you to repent for not trusting God? Do you take time daily to confess all of the ways you haven't trusted Him? What steps are you taking to trust that the same God who created and saved you is worthy of your confidence?

YIELD

Israel was faced with a choice to trust God. Will you trust Him?

In light of Scripture and based on your responses,
quiet yourself before the Lord and spend a few moments in prayer.

GOD'S ETERNALITY AND HUMANITY'S TEMPORALITY

Read Psalm 90:3-6.

In this passage Moses' prayer transitioned from affirming God's eternality to confessing humanity's temporality. Scholar and commentator Allen Ross notes the contrast between the previous and current passages: "God outlasts the most enduring things in creation (v. 2), but humans return to dust (v. 3)."[3] This contrast is further evidenced in the direct link between Moses' words in verse 3 ("Return, descendants of Adam") and God's words in Genesis 3:19 ("You are dust, and you will return to dust").[4] Indeed, humankind is nothing in comparison to the eternal God. He raised Adam from the dust, and He will return his descendants to the dust.

Psalm 90 reminds us that God won't allow humankind to continue in flagrant sin. We're on the earth for a brief time. Moses clarified this point when he said:

> A thousand years
> are like yesterday that passes by,
> like a few hours of the night.
> **PSALM 90:4**

Moses meant that what seems like forever "is nothing to someone who is eternal."[5] In comparison to God, "human life is so brief that it's almost insignificant."[6] Like Moses' wilderness generation, all flesh will perish.

Death, however, comes not just for the unrighteous. Commenting on the extended simile in verses 5-6, Ross insightfully contends that "humans may flourish for a time, a brief time, but in the end their life is ended and they wither away."[7] We should all consider our brief lives, not just those of the wicked. One day, like the wilderness generation, our bodies will wither and die, and we'll stand before God, called to give an account for our sins. Moses addressed the implications of this prospect in the next portion of the psalm.

22

PRAYER

Enter this time with your Bible and your heart open.
Based on the truths of Scripture, answer the following
questions and let them lead you to a time of prayer.

PRAISE

Psalm 90 reminds us of our frailty. When have you thanked the eternal God that He has chosen to care for such a feeble creature as you?

REPENT

What changes about your perspective when you take time to consider that your days are numbered? Have you considered that the only reason you have breath and substance is that God has chosen to sustain you? Do you realize that if you've trusted in Christ, the same God who sustains you now will also do so in eternity?

APPLY

What will it take for you to come to grips with your frailty and thank God for His care for you? What changes when you understand that God has chosen to save weak people who realize their need for a Savior?

YIELD

Israel had the choice to depend on God for salvation in the wilderness. We also have a similar choice to make. Will you trust that your only hope in the present and in the future is the salvation that comes through the God who sent His Son to die on a cross and rise from the grave in your place for your sins?

In light of Scripture and based on your responses,
quiet yourself before the Lord and spend a few moments in prayer.

GOD'S WRATH TOWARD SINNERS

Read Psalm 90:7-12.

While wandering in the wilderness, Moses was an eyewitness to Israel's rebellion. Events such as the golden calf (see Ex. 32) and grumbling for food and water (see Ex. 16–17) were just the tip of the iceberg; there were others (see Num. 14), even events not recorded in the Pentateuch. Because of such wickedness, Moses acknowledged in Psalm 90 that God was angry with His people and that they, in turn, were "terrified" by His "wrath" (v. 7). There was nowhere to escape from God. Not even their "secret sins" went unnoticed, for all of their iniquities were evident "in the light" of God's "presence" (v. 8).

Like the wilderness generation, we all deserve God's wrath. David rightly acknowledged that "there is no one who does good" (Ps. 14:1; 53:1; see Rom. 3:12). Let's not fool ourselves. Let's stop pointing a finger at the person in the courtroom giving an account for his sins on live television. Certainly he deserves his day of reckoning, but we must understand that we'll all stand before the Judge of the universe (see Rev. 20:11-15). He knows we too are guilty, committing the same sins for which we judge others. Paul affirmed:

> Every one of you who judges is without excuse.
> For when you judge another, you condemn yourself,
> since you, the judge, do the same things.
> **ROMANS 2:1**

Surely we stand condemned, just like the criminal on television. God's righteous anger burns against us. What are we to do?

Our desperation is even more evident when we consider the brevity of human life. Moses claimed that even people who live long lives of seventy or eighty years "pass quickly" and "fly away" (Ps. 90:10). Simply put, human life is like a flashing light in comparison to the eternal God. Do we understand that we'll give an account—all of us, not just rapists and murderers? Do we understand that we'll soon face God, whose wrath burns because of our iniquity?

PRAYER

Enter this time with your Bible and your heart open.
Based on the truths of Scripture, answer the following
questions and let them lead you to a time of prayer.

PRAISE

God sees our sin. Do you praise God for not striking you down, as He did the Israelites in the wilderness for their iniquity against Him? Do you thank God because the events in the wilderness "were written for our instruction" (1 Cor. 10:11) so that we can turn to Jesus and live?

REPENT

One day you'll stand before Jesus (see Rev. 20:11-15). How are you like the sinful Israelites who needed to repent? Do you know you'll be able to stand before Jesus and declared righteous only if you've trusted that on the cross He paid the penalty for your sins (see Rom. 3; 1 Cor. 15)?

APPLY

If you've never come to grips with your sins, even those concealed in private, consider that God sees what you do; He knows what lies in your heart. Have you considered that you won't be able to justify such sins before Him? Have you considered repenting and trusting in Jesus?

YIELD

The Israelites had the opportunity to repent and trust in God, but they didn't, dying in the wilderness. What do you need to learn from their mistakes? Will you repent and live?

In light of Scripture and based on your responses,
quiet yourself before the Lord and spend a few moments in prayer.

LONGING FOR GOD'S SALVATION

Read Psalm 90:13–14.

Moses began these verses with a question: "How long" would God be angry with His people? He then prayed, "Turn and have compassion on your servants" (v. 13). The request for God to turn was a prayer to restore His compassion and mercy to the Israelites.[8]

Moses petitioned for Israel to experience a new season of mercy and compassion by appealing to God's "faithful love" embodied in His covenant with Abraham, which promised to give His people a land where they would experience rest (v. 14; see Gen. 12; 15; 17). Though the Israelites were distressed, God's covenant with Abraham gave them hope of living in a land of blessing. Moses' appeal to God's covenant faithfulness was meant to move the Lord to deliver His people from the wilderness and into the promised place of blessing, where they would dwell forever.

The Scriptures record that Moses died without leading the people into the land. Joshua eventually led them into Canaan, yet because of their sin, God later exiled them from the land (see 1 Sam.–2 Chron.). The hope for a promised land, however, wasn't lost, for the prophets anticipated the inheritance of a re-created world (see Ezek. 36–37; Isa. 40–66), fulfilling God's promises to Abraham.

Even though Moses never entered the promised land, he died satisfied, for God allowed him to see the land the Israelites would one day possess (see Num. 27:12). Moses, however, had a large enough vision to see beyond the land, knowing it was only a type of the renewed world in which God's people would dwell. After all, God had promised His people, "I will give your offspring all these lands, and all the nations of the earth will be blessed by your offspring" (Gen. 26:4). God's promise always had cosmic proportions. Canaan was only a type of the better land. So when Moses saw the land, he looked beyond it, envisioning the better promised land God's people would inherit. Then he could die a happy man.

Unless Jesus returns soon, we'll all die in the present wilderness of sin and death. Our goal is to anticipate the renewed world God has promised to the faithful descendants of Abraham, the place where Moses' eyes truly gazed (see Rom. 4; 8; Gal. 3; Rev. 21–22).

PRAYER

Enter this time with your Bible and your heart open.
Based on the truths of Scripture, answer the following
questions and let them lead you to a time of prayer.

PRAISE

God could have chosen to leave us in our present sinful wilderness. If you've trusted in the death and resurrection of Christ, why should you regularly thank Him for saving you? If you haven't trusted in Christ, why not trust Him today?

REPENT

In what or whom are you trusting to deliver you from your circumstances?

APPLY

What will it take for you to look only to Christ for salvation?

YIELD

After reading Psalm 90, do you know that you have the same hope as Moses: the hope of deliverance through Christ into a renewed creation?

In light of Scripture and based on your responses,
quiet yourself before the Lord and spend a few moments in prayer.

GOD'S SALVATION WILL COME

Read Psalm 90:15-17.

Although Moses saw the blessed land that awaits God's people, we must concede that it's hard to gaze into future blessing when you're stuck in present hardship. The Israelites had firsthand knowledge of this experience, for their adversity in the wilderness had lasted for what may have seemed like an eternity. So when Moses requested that God make His people "rejoice for as many days as you have humbled us, for as many years as we have seen adversity" (v. 15), he was asking God to grant His people rejoicing in a measure equal to their sorrow.

Adversity has a knack for slowing down time, making us think we'll perpetually suffer. For example, people who struggle with depression can describe prolonged periods of darkness, longing for the light of morning. Although I can't prove that Moses was depressed, I can affirm that he knew darkness. He knew pain. From his protracted anguish he prayed to God, longing for a time of flourishing.

Moses also prayed for "the favor of the Lord" and to see God "establish ... the work of our hands" (v. 17). Moses' petition was "an appeal to God to enable them [Israel] to have a productive life, a life that has value."[9] Moses' appeal was firmly grounded in the promises of the Abrahamic covenant in the Genesis narrative, where God promised that His people would live in a land of permanent blessing. Isaiah called this place the new heavens and earth, where God's "chosen ones will fully enjoy the work of their hands" (Isa. 65:22), where Israel "will not labor without success or bear children destined for disaster, for they will be a people blessed by the LORD along with their descendants" (v. 23). Once again, this is the place Moses saw when he looked beyond Canaan.

If believers continue to hope in Christ, we'll see in person what Moses saw from a distance. In that place we'll be delivered from our suffering; oppressors will be crushed, and the meek will be lifted up (see Ps. 37; Matt. 5:5). Is that what your heart yearns for? Is that what your soul longs to experience? This is what awaits you as a Christian: your eternal home, where you'll find rest in the arms of Jesus.

PRAYER

Enter this time with your Bible and your heart open.
Based on the truths of Scripture, answer the following
questions and let them lead you to a time of prayer.

PRAISE

Are you enduring what seems like an endless period of darkness? Are you experiencing a prolonged period of pain? Praise God, who will one day deliver you from all struggles.

REPENT

Why do you focus on your struggles? Why might God want something better for you?

APPLY

Didn't Moses look forward to what awaited God's people? Why not, then, look forward to the renewed world of blessing that awaits you?

YIELD

Who are some people in your life who need to be told or reminded about the blessed creation reserved for the followers of Christ? Why not comfort them with this truth?

In light of Scripture and based on your responses,
quiet yourself before the Lord and spend a few moments in prayer.

Welcome to group session 2 of *Praying at the Crossroads.*

Use the following questions to begin the session.

Have you ever faced a difficult time when you couldn't figure out why God was allowing your difficulties? If so, how did you pray?

Have you ever felt that you were praying too much about something? If so, what was the situation?

This Bible study is about praying at the crossroads—at pivotal moments in life when our wisdom is insufficient and our power is weak. Seeking the face of God at those times is not only the right move but also the imperative move. To take a step at the crossroads without God's leadership can be foolish.

On the other hand, sometimes the right move is to pray briefly and then act swiftly. That was the case with Joshua and the Hebrews after their battle for the city of Ai. They had experienced great victories in crossing the Jordan River and conquering the city of Jericho, but that wasn't the case with the battle for Ai. Instead, they experienced defeat for the first time in the promised land, and that defeat was devastating. At least thirty-six of the Hebrew warriors lost their lives.

Joshua, the new leader of the Hebrews, immediately sought the Lord for understanding and direction. Grief overwhelmed him as he prayed. His prayer, though, wasn't long. God interrupted him.

Use these statements to follow along as you watch video session 2.

We're taught to pray reactively.

God rolled the water back as He paved the way for the people to take the land He had given them.

For the first time in the promised land, the people experienced defeat.

Sometimes when we think about praying at the crossroads, the best we can do is say, "God, I understand why this has happened, so I'm just crying out to you."

God said, "Get up. There's sin in the camp, and you've got to take care of this." Sometimes it's easier for us to speak to God than it is to deal with the issues at hand.

Prayer is right. Prayer is our strategy. We must turn to God.

There are other times when God says, "All right, you prayed. Get up. Get to work."

Video sessions available at lifeway.com/prayingatthecrossroads or with a subscription to smallgroup.com

DISCUSS

Use the following questions to discuss the video teaching.

Read Joshua 7.

What tragedies are described in this account? What caused these tragedies?

The Bible calls us to "pray constantly" (1 Thess. 5:17). Jesus also taught us to pray before temptation rather than during or after it (see Matt. 6:13). Dr. Lawless pointed out on the video, however, that much of our praying is reactionary praying rather than proactive praying. We don't know for certain, but it's possible that Joshua's prayer about the battle of Ai was only reactive.

Reactive praying in itself isn't wrong, especially when life unexpectedly becomes a struggle. None of us plan for a defeat as the Hebrews experienced at Ai. On the other hand, offering only reactive prayers isn't a sign of a healthy prayer life.

Would you describe your prayer life as proactive or reactive?

If it's the latter, how could you change your prayer pattern to pray more proactively?

The people of God suffered their first defeat in the promised land at Ai, and Joshua, their leader, didn't immediately know the reason behind the defeat. Both his grief and his questioning are apparent in his prayer in Joshua 7:6-9. It seemed to him that God had allowed the warriors of Ai to defeat the Israelites, and that prospect created a crisis of faith for him.

Are you comfortable talking to God the way Joshua did in verses 7-9? Why or why not?

When was the most recent time you didn't understand why something happened, but you didn't talk to God about it?

Joshua prayed with great passion over the loss at Ai, but God wouldn't allow him to stay on his knees. Sin had created the problem, and the leader and the people had to address that sin. Confrontation was in order. Sometimes our prayer might simply be preparation that's quickly followed by action, especially when we already know what we should do in the first place. Knowing when to pray and when to act, though, isn't always easy.

In what situations might God say to us, "Pray, but then get up quickly and get to work"?

The account of the judgment of Achan and his family is a difficult one. The judgment seems severe, but it's a reminder that God expects His people to be holy. Particularly when they first entered the promised land, He wanted them to know immediately that He expected them to be different from the other inhabitants. We see the same kind of judgment on Nadab and Abihu when God first instituted the sacrificial system (see Lev. 10:1-3) and on Ananias and Sapphira in the early days of the church (see Acts 5:1-11). God graciously doesn't judge us all this way, but He still demands our holiness. Taking our sin lightly isn't an option.

How can these truths affect the way you pray about your temptations and sin?

How important is it for other believers to pray for you as you respond to temptation?

GROUP PRAYER

Use the following PRAY framework to pray together as a group.

In light of what we've studied today, pray together as a group, using the following prompts to guide your experience together. You'll repeat this exercise at the end of each day's personal study. Use the biblical prayer we studied to guide your own. Read each prompt aloud and encourage group members to lift up prayers based on these prompts silently or aloud, depending on their comfort level.

PRAISE *God for who He is and what He has done.*

God is a holy God who requires holiness, but He also makes it possible through Christ for sinful people to follow Him. Praise Him for His holiness and His grace.

REPENT *of unconfessed sins and accept Christ's forgiveness.*

Achan's sin cost him, his family, and the people of Israel. It's also not clear whether he ever truly repented of his sin. Recognizing that your sin affects others too, genuinely confess any sin in your life.

APPLY *the truths you've learned by committing to action.*

Joshua prayed, but God told him to get up and root out the sin in the camp. You may already know something God expects you to do, but you haven't yet been obedient. Pray about it and commit to do what God has required.

YIELD *your life to God's will and kind providence.*

Following God requires confessing and repenting of our own sin. At times it also requires confronting someone else's sin. Pray about your willingness to take both of these actions, knowing that each can be painful.

Close by praying for specific requests that arose during the session.

SIN, JUDGMENT, AND PRAYER

Read Joshua 7:1.

The story of the Hebrews was a roller coaster of obedience and disobedience. Some forty years before, another generation had come to the brink of the promised land. Moses' spies had explored the land, and the majority had cowered in fear, placing more weight on the size of the enemy than on the power of their God (see Num. 13). The cost of their disobedience was heavy: an entire generation died in the wilderness.

God then raised up Joshua as the new leader of the next generation, and they obeyed his directions to enter the promised land. They followed the priests and the ark of the covenant into the Jordan River as God rolled back its waters. They "hurried across" the Jordan (Josh. 4:10), set up stones to commemorate the miracle, circumcised the new generation, and observed the Passover for the first time in the land.

Next the walled city of Jericho stood in their way as the Israelites pressed into Canaan, but God had a plan for them. They were to walk around the wall, blow their trumpets, and shout as He supernaturally collapsed the city walls. He commanded them, however, not to take any spoils of the city for themselves (see 6:18-19). If any Israelite kept anything for himself, the entire camp of the Hebrews would pay a price.

And that's exactly what happened. One man, Achan, took a cloak, gold, and silver and hid them in his tent (see 7:21). However, today's reading says the Israelites sinned, not just Achan, and God's anger burned against all of them.

This story reminds believers today that none of us sin in isolation; rather, we're so connected as the people of God that our sin affects not only us but also our families and our churches.

Our obedience brings God's affirmation, but our disobedience brings God's judgment. Sometimes, in fact, our disobedience requires that our spiritual leaders intercede for us with great heartache and passion, as we'll see with Joshua. At other times we're the ones who intercede for others.

PRAYER

Enter this time with your Bible and your heart open.
Based on the truths of Scripture, answer the following
questions and let them lead you to a time of prayer.

PRAISE

Have you spent much time thinking about the victories God has given you in life? When was the most recent time you simply praised Him for leading you into victory?

REPENT

Achan's sin was private, but it affected all of the people. What sin in your life might be affecting your family and your church? How might it be affecting them?

APPLY

Sin can be not only sins of commission (doing things we shouldn't do) but also sins of omission (not doing things we know we should do). What are your sins of omission? Bible reading? Prayer? Evangelism? Giving? Forgiving others?

YIELD

Today's Scripture reminds us that sin has consequences. One of those consequences is that sin hinders our prayers (see Isa. 59:1-2). Are you willing to spend time in repentance today to remove barriers to your prayers?

In light of Scripture and based on your responses,
quiet yourself before the Lord and spend a few moments in prayer.

OVERCONFIDENCE AND PRAYERLESSNESS

Read Joshua 7:2-5.

"Go up and scout the land," Joshua told the men (v. 2). Ai was the next city for the Hebrews to conquer, and Joshua sent spies to investigate the city's resources. Unlike the spies Moses had sent into the land decades before, these spies were confident the Hebrews could take the city. They saw only a few enemy forces, so they saw no need for the Israelites to send many warriors into battle. Only two or three thousand would be sufficient, they thought.

However, tragedy soon resulted. The forces of Ai routed the Israelite army, killed about three dozen of them, and chased them for some distance. In the past the native people of Canaan had "lost heart" when they heard about God's power (2:11), but now it was the people of God who became discouraged. Unexpected defeat broke their spirits.

Despite the fact that God alone had miraculously led them through the Red Sea and Jericho, the people were likely far too confident in their own ability as they attacked Ai. Moses' spies had underestimated the power of God to give them the land, but Joshua's spies overestimated their own power to take the city. We can't know for certain, but it's also possible that the Hebrews entered Ai without praying and seeking God's guidance and protection. We know they later made bad decisions without praying (see 9:14), and they may have made the same mistake at Ai.

If that's the case, the first recorded prayer we have about Ai takes place after their defeat. Praying after the fact might seem illogical to us, but we often pray the same way. Think about it. We tend to pray because we need God's help rather than because we simply want to talk to God. Many of us try to fix first, then pray only if we must. We climb our own mountains as far as we can climb them, and we start praying only when we can climb no more. Our prayerlessness reveals our overconfidence.

PRAYER

Enter this time with your Bible and your heart open.
Based on the truths of Scripture, answer the following
questions and let them lead you to a time of prayer.

PRAISE

Joshua 7 would be even more tragic if Joshua 8 didn't record God's giving the Hebrews a second chance to defeat Ai. Have you praised God lately for second chances?

REPENT

Are you overconfident? If someone evaluated your self-confidence based on your prayer life, what would he or she conclude?

APPLY

One problem with overconfidence is that we don't recognize it until it's too late. Who in your life has your permission to point out any overconfidence?

YIELD

What's your level of confidence today? Have you fully placed your confidence in God?

In light of Scripture and based on your responses,
quiet yourself before the Lord and spend a few moments in prayer.

QUESTIONS AND PRAYER

Read Joshua 7:6–9.

Imagine the scene. Joshua was God's called man to lead His people. God had promised that He would be with Joshua just as He had been with Moses (see 1:5) and that He would give the Israelites every part of the land on which Joshua walked (see 1:3). Indeed, He had worked miracles that couldn't be denied, rolling back the waters of the Jordan River and collapsing the walls of the city of Jericho. God had even made Himself known to Joshua as the commander of the Lord's army (see 5:13-15) prior to the battle for Jericho. Now, though, everything was different.

The armies of God had been defeated at Ai. Thirty-six deaths may not have seemed like many out of three thousand warriors, but they had lost no one in the battle for Jericho. The deaths were signs of God's displeasure, and Joshua had no idea what had caused His anger. His anguish over defeat was so great that he and the elders fell on their faces before the Lord, covered their heads with ashes, and tore their clothes (common signs of grief in that day). And Joshua took the right course of action: he sought the Lord in prayer.

The questions of Joshua's prayer, however, reveal his struggle. He was reverent, but he questioned why God brought His people into the land at all if He intended for them to be defeated. Why not just let them stay on the other side of the Jordan? And what would other nations say about God's great name if they defeated God's people? Joshua's prayer seems to have been the intercession of a man who questioned God's willingness to keep His covenant but who also didn't consider the possibility of sin in the Israelite camp.

Turning to the Lord in prayer in times of defeat is the right move. He's God—the Creator of all, the One whose shoulders are broad enough to bear the weight of our questions. We must be prepared, however, for an answer we hadn't expected. The problem might be hidden sin.

PRAYER

Enter this time with your Bible and your heart open.
Based on the truths of Scripture, answer the following
questions and let them lead you to a time of prayer.

PRAISE

Are you trusting God with all of your questions, including those that wonder about His care? Do you ask all of your questions and then praise Him for being willing to hear them?

REPENT

Maybe your sin isn't questioning God but being unwilling to give your questions to Him. What questions—even those that reveal your struggle—do you need to ask Him today?

APPLY

If you've identified questions you want to ask God in prayer, have you asked them yet? What keeps you from doing so?

YIELD

Do you genuinely believe God wants to hear your questions and your faith struggles?

In light of Scripture and based on your responses,
quiet yourself before the Lord and spend a few moments in prayer.

GRIEF, INTERRUPTIONS, AND PRAYER

Read Joshua 7:10-15.

Has God ever surprised you by His answer to your prayer? Joshua likely didn't expect God's clear, dramatic response to his intercession on behalf of the people: "Stand up!" God said. "Why have you fallen facedown?" (v. 10). In essence God was saying, "You've prayed enough. There's something you need to do." Sin was in the camp, and Joshua had some tough work to carry out. It was time to confront the sinners.

Not only was Joshua to recognize the sin problem, but he was also to arise and call the people to consecrate themselves in preparation for God's judgment. Somebody had taken spoils from Jericho, and that person was to be rooted out and killed. Such a dramatic judgment showed that God wouldn't tolerate sin among His people in the promised land. The Israelites had finally entered the land, and at this pivotal crossroads God clearly and dramatically established His standards.

Joshua's praying wasn't wrong, but praying alone wouldn't resolve the issue. Nothing short of confrontation and discipline would be sufficient. In fact, praying may have been the easiest part of this task. Talking to God—even questioning God as Joshua did—was probably easier than calling out Achan and leading the people to judge him and his family through burning. The prayer closet may have seemed safer than the judgment hall, but Joshua's brief conversation with God necessitated a more difficult conversation with Achan. Ignoring judgment on Achan and his family wasn't an option.

Our circumstances are seldom as dramatic as those in this story, but sometimes we too need to pray briefly and act quickly on God's revealed will. For example, we don't need to pray long before deciding to share the gospel with an unbelieving neighbor. Deciding whether to give cheerfully to God's work (see 2 Cor. 9:7), to minister to the needy (see Matt. 25:31-46), to make disciples of all nations (see Matt. 28:18-20), or to be grateful in everything (see 1 Thess. 5:18) shouldn't require lengthy times of prayer. We know what we need to do; we just need to do it.

PRAYER

Enter this time with your Bible and your heart open.
Based on the truths of Scripture, answer the following
questions and let them lead you to a time of prayer.

PRAISE

Has God used other people to confront you in your sin? Do you praise Him for others who love you that much?

REPENT

We can't read today's text without seeing the seriousness of sin. How seriously do you view your own sin?

APPLY

Do you need to lovingly confront someone about his or her sin? Are you ready to act after you've prayed?

YIELD

In what area of your life do you need to get up and act? When will you take the first step of obedience?

In light of Scripture and based on your responses,
quiet yourself before the Lord and spend a few moments in prayer.

CONFESSION AND PRAYER

Read Joshua 7:16-26.

Sometimes our "repentance" is something less than actual repentance, and that appears to be the case with Achan. He had followed the same pattern of sin Adam and Eve did: he saw something he wanted, coveted it, took it, and then concealed it (see vv. 20-21). Having violated God's covenant by taking spoils, lying about his action, and hiding the articles among his own belongings, he didn't seem to have been genuinely sorrowful about his choices.

Notice the process Joshua followed to identify Achan. Progressively, Joshua brought forth all of the tribes and narrowed them to Judah. Then he called out the clans of Judah and narrowed them to the clan of the Zerahites. Next he worked through each man of the Zerahites to narrow the clan to the family of Zabdi. Finally, he faced each man in the family of Zabdi, ultimately coming face-to-face with Achan. Joshua said to him, "My son, give glory to the LORD, the God of Israel, and make a confession to him" (v. 19).

Achan admitted his sin but only after the spotlight was shone on him. The detailed process of identifying him was likely God's way of giving him numerous opportunities to repent and confess, but he didn't do so. He didn't admit his sin when Joshua was one step closer to identifying him by narrowing the tribes to Judah. Nor did he confess as the progression through the clans and families tightened the noose around him. Perhaps fear caused him to be honest as Joshua ultimately confronted him, but his previous silence suggests that his heart was hardened.

Maybe today is a crossroads for you. You may be a believer, but you have sin in your life that harms your relationship with God and hinders your prayers (see Ps. 66:18-20; Isa. 59:1-2) even as you're learning to pray through this study. Or it's possible that you've never entered a personal relationship with Jesus. If that's the case, turn from your sin and trust Jesus to save you. Today's crossroads can be your first step toward eternal life.

PRAYER

Enter this time with your Bible and your heart open.
Based on the truths of Scripture, answer the following
questions and let them lead you to a time of prayer.

PRAISE

"If we confess our sins, [God] is faithful and righteous to forgive us our sins and to cleanse us from all unrighteousness" (1 John 1:9). Do you believe that truth?

REPENT

Does your confession ever suggest that you're not serious about your repentance? Have you turned from your sin to trust Jesus as your Savior?

APPLY

There's a place for confessing our sins to God and to other believers (see Jas. 5:16). Do you have someone who can pray with you about overcoming your sin?

YIELD

Disobedience affects our prayers. Is today a crossroads for you regarding your sin and your praying?

In light of Scripture and based on your responses,
quiet yourself before the Lord and spend a few moments in prayer.

Welcome to group session 3 of *Praying at the Crossroads.*

Use the following questions to begin the session.

How do you view people who hold leadership positions? Have you ever stopped to consider how lonely leadership can be?

What positions of influence do you hold? How can you use your influence for the gospel?

Leadership can often seem to be a solitary role. As we observe the shepherds of our church or organization, we see them through the lens of hierarchy. We might even assume they make major resolutions with only their own faculties and abilities; in doing so, they put everything on the line, hoping for the best outcome but resolute to shoulder the blame if necessary.

Such solitude can give us pause. Almost all of us are in positions of influence, and when the time comes for us to take the lead, we often experience a fight-or-flight response. We might act immediately, thinking we can take on the world in our own strength. Or we can try to avoid responsibility, certain that anything we do will end in defeat.

The prayers of a faithful leader can reveal a different picture. Leadership under a Creator who works on behalf of His people nurtures attitudes like humility and thankfulness.

The Lord hears and responds when His people call out to Him. The question is, Do we long to hear from Him? Do we initiate a prayerful dialogue with God before we're broken by circumstances?

Use these statements to follow along as you watch video session 3.

All of us are called to be leaders because that's what it means to make disciples.

Sometimes it can seem so overwhelming and we can become so afraid that we forget where we're supposed to put our hope.

Everyone was doing their own thing exactly as they thought it should be, when it was the complete opposite of what the Lord had for them.

Deborah knew and understood what it means to lead in the sight of the Lord.

Deborah had led the Israelites, knowing that victory was certain because God was leading the way.

Deborah's prayer was one of reflection, displaying hope in front of the Israelites.

Deborah pointed to the One who had delivered them, and she spoke of leadership from the beginning.

The true gift of Deborah's leadership was in her hope.

When God calls us to step up and lead, He's calling us to lean on Him— to assume that the mission is His, that the victory has been won, and that He's going out before us.

Deborah's prayer shows us something of her character, something of her heart, and an example.

We see in Deborah the heart of a leader who points to something bigger than herself.

As Christians, we are called to be leaders because we are leading the world to look at the true and living God and what He has done in His Son.

Video sessions available at lifeway.com/prayingatthecrossroads or with a subscription to smallgroup.com

DISCUSS

Use the following questions to discuss the video teaching.

Read Judges 4–5.

How would you describe the Israelite's relationship with the Lord at this point in history?

The cyclical narratives in Judges begin in a similar way: "The Israelites again did what was evil in the sight of the LORD" (4:1). After Moses and Joshua, the tribal leaders lacked a moral compass. The people of Israel, left to their own devices, repeatedly turned to evil. The Lord then gave them over to their enemies. When they cried out to Him, He delivered them, working through judges and leaders. This pattern was reenacted seven times throughout the Book of Judges.

How might our relationship with God positively or negatively affect our prayer life?

What differentiated the leadership of Deborah from the leadership of Barak?

Something is different about the story in Judges 4–5 because of a special individual: "Deborah, a prophetess and the wife of Lappidoth, was judging Israel at that time" (4:4). Deborah's credibility is established early in chapter 4, and the remainder of the narrative enhances her godly reputation.

Barak, on the other hand, ran from the role of a leader. We don't know when or where the call came to him, but we know it did. Deborah summoned him to deploy an army to fight against Jabin's commander, Sisera. In some ways we can understand his fear, because anyone under the intimidation of an oppressive regime would be afraid to challenge the dictator.

When we feel ill-equipped for the task at hand, why can it be beneficial to stop and pray?

When have you received both confidence and strength through prayer?

Barak believed he could disregard God's call, but Deborah summoned him with the fact that she knew his secret. He couldn't run from hope. Victory had been assured, and there was no room for fear. But even as she challenged him, Barak was afraid to stand without her, saying, "If you will go with me, I will go. But if you will not go with me, I will not go" (v. 8).

Barak's fear was that he would stand alone, when in reality the Lord had promised His presence from the beginning. Barak paid a hefty price for his shaken confidence. His dependence on another person ensured that credit wouldn't be his. Deborah had to tell him, "I will gladly go with you, … but you will receive no honor on the road you are about to take, because the LORD will sell Sisera to a woman" (v. 9). The irony of this statement is that Deborah was prepared to take whatever honor she might receive and hand it to the Lord.

> *Whom might you need to encourage in his or her confidence and service to the Lord? When will you reach out to that person?*

When the battle came, God's unseen hand clearly led the charge. Even when Deborah pushed Barak to act, she did so by reminding him that victory was certain: "Go! This is the day the LORD has handed Sisera over to you. Hasn't the LORD gone before you?" (v. 14). This encouragement was enough, and Barak took his army down the mountain.

We can't know for certain, but all we've seen of Barak's character implies that he must have been trembling with fear as he went out in front of those ten thousand men. He was a reluctant commander, but the assurance of victory and the confidence of Deborah had finally moved his feet. Ultimately, though, the real movement came from the God of Israel: "The LORD threw Sisera, all his charioteers, and all his army into a panic before Barak's assault" (v. 15).

> *How does the practice of prayer help build our confidence in the power and promised deliverance of our God?*

GROUP PRAYER

Use the following PRAY framework to pray together as a group.

In light of what we've studied today, pray together as a group, using the following prompts to guide your experience together. You'll repeat this exercise at the end of each day's personal study. Use the biblical prayer we studied to guide your own. Read each prompt aloud and encourage group members to lift up prayers based on these prompts silently or aloud, depending on their comfort level.

PRAISE *God for who He is and what He has done.*
God is always there for us even when we feel as though He isn't. The limits of our strength and confidence are meant to lead us to the boundless store of power available in God. Express the gratitude that comes from serving a God who isn't limited.

REPENT *of unconfessed sins and accept Christ's forgiveness.*
The Lord has placed a call on our lives to follow Him in obedience. Anything less than doing as God says is disobedience. Ask for and receive God's forgiveness for past or current disobedience.

APPLY *the truths you've learned by committing to action.*
Spend time praying for a team or group that needs courageous leadership from you, whether it's your family, business, or church ministry.

YIELD *your life to God's will and kind providence.*
"Out of sight, out of mind" might work in theory but not in practice in a relationship with the omniscient God. Commit yourself this moment to do all God asks, to cast your fears on Him, and to step forward in obedience.

Close by praying for specific requests that arose during the session.

HAVE CONFIDENCE IN THE LORD

Read Judges 4.

Can you imagine what the battle must have been like for Barak? He had been terrified from the beginning of this account, and the deliverance came right before his eyes. There would have been no question in his or Deborah's mind that they had been called to a mission that God would accomplish for them.

When Sisera fled on foot, God delivered him into the hand of Jael. The prophecy that Barak would receive no honor materialized when he found Sisera dead at the hands of a courageous woman playing one small role in the story. The contrast is stark. Jael was alone, and she knew what Sisera could do to her. But she acted strategically and swiftly. Barak, finally empowered to pursue his enemy, was too late to finish the job.

But Barak and Deborah weren't to be the stars of the story, regardless of the way Sisera's command ended. The writer of Judges was clear:

> That day God subdued Jabin king of Canaan before the Israelites. The power of the Israelites continued to increase against Jabin king of Canaan until they destroyed him.
> **JUDGES 4:23-24**

It was after this proclamation of God's great works for His children that Deborah's prayer sprang forth. She didn't take lightly or grasp for herself this moment of victory and affirmation of her leadership. She pointed all glory outward and to the One who had secured the people's hope.

We often look to God for help and deliverance, lean on Him in the most challenging moments, and then take glory for ourselves when we've accomplished our goals. Our memories become warped as we look back and place ourselves at the center of victory.

PRAYER

Enter this time with your Bible and your heart open.
Based on the truths of Scripture, answer the following
questions and let them lead you to a time of prayer.

PRAISE

Our culture presses us to take credit for all of our victories. The Scriptures present a different model. When you endure one of life's battles, do you praise God?

REPENT

Have you succumbed to that temptation and robbed the Lord of the credit and glory due His name? Who gets credit for your victories?

APPLY

Barak's path would have been easier if he had acknowledged and embraced the Lord's deliverance sooner. When you experience deliverance, do you recognize the presence of God? How do you acknowledge what He has done?

YIELD

God actively goes ahead of you in your daily life. How do you anticipate His action and seek Him both before and after it?

In light of Scripture and based on your responses,
quiet yourself before the Lord and spend a few moments in prayer.

THE VICTORY IS THE LORD'S

> **Read Judges 5:1-5.**

The song of Deborah is a song of faith, understanding leadership as a call to action that's deeply connected to prayer and praise for the Lord. The triumphs of the people came from the actions of the God of Israel, and at the beginning of Deborah's song she properly attributed the victory to the Lord (see v. 2).

Deborah and Barak placed the honor of the leaders at the feet of the Lord. He was the One who positioned them, gave them strength, and called them to act. They took no personal credit for their actions. They believed in God's promise to deliver, they acted in accordance with that certainty, and their final call of prayer placed the Lord at the center of the victory.

In moments of heroism or accomplishment today, well-known people in our culture often thank God for His help and strength. In cynical moments we can treat these statements with suspicion. We wonder whether they really mean what they're saying, because we assume they surely want to take credit for themselves. But we see in Deborah's prayer that giving credit to God is exactly the example we should follow. We don't struggle on our own, and we don't prevail on our own. And in times of success, we must acknowledge the Lord's provision.

Deborah proclaimed that the battle belonged to the Lord:

> LORD, when you came from Seir,
> when you marched from the fields of Edom,
> the earth trembled,
> the skies poured rain,
> and the clouds poured water.
> The mountains melted before the LORD,
> even Sinai, before the LORD, the God of Israel.
> **JUDGES 5:4-5**

The people who had been trying to live on their own, doing what was evil, were now seeing that the Lord was going before them. They had forgotten Him, but He hadn't forgotten them. And in this moment Deborah pointed them to the Creator of the universe, whose universe followed His will. She gave all praise to Him.

PRAYER

Enter this time with your Bible and your heart open.
Based on the truths of Scripture, answer the following
questions and let them lead you to a time of prayer.

PRAISE

Every victory gives us an opportunity to give God honor and glory for securing success. Do the people with whom you share close relationships with ever hear you praise God for His help?

REPENT

Failure to acknowledge God is sin. When God goes before You, do you forget Him, or do you acknowledge His provision?

APPLY

How will you God honor this week for your successes? How could you help people see God more clearly through your life?

YIELD

Deborah didn't shrink from the mission, but she always knew who was doing the real work. We can live the same way. How can you live in light of God's work on your behalf?

In light of Scripture and based on your responses,
quiet yourself before the Lord and spend a few moments in prayer.

THE GLORY BELONGS TO THE LORD

Read Judges 5:6–11.

The part of the story that seems to be about Deborah still tells a story of God's faithfulness to His people. Before God brought forth a deliverer, the common way of life had ceased to exist, and God's people threw themselves further and further into idolatry and wickedness. This passage doesn't credit Deborah's leadership, character, and appearance on the scene to her willingness or her ability but to God's grace in providing a deliverer.

While acknowledging her role in the nation's ascension, Deborah didn't keep the glory for herself but proclaimed:

> My heart is with the leaders of Israel,
> with the volunteers of the people.
> Blessed be the LORD!
> You who ride on white donkeys,
> who sit on saddle blankets,
> and who travel on the road, give praise!
> Let them tell the righteous acts of the LORD,
> the righteous deeds of his warriors in Israel,
> with the voices of the singers at the watering places.
> **JUDGES 5:9–11**

At times we can see how the Lord has used us in situations, particularly in moments of leadership. When that happens, pride knocks on the door of our hearts, tempting us to claim that the credit belongs to us alone. Deborah's example shows us another way. Deborah never saw this as her mission. She knew she was merely playing a role in God's mission.

PRAYER

Enter this time with your Bible and your heart open.
Based on the truths of Scripture, answer the following
questions and let them lead you to a time of prayer.

PRAISE

Have you moved beyond a blessing from the Lord without a season of praise
and worship? Take a moment to pause, as Deborah did, and exalt God for
His faithful providence.

REPENT

Are you self-reliant or prideful? Do you take the blessings of the Lord
for granted, as if you knew He would act in a way that would benefit you?

APPLY

How can you begin to see yourself as playing a role in God's greater mission?
What might that role look like at this stage in your life?

YIELD

God is always the main character in the story line of our lives. How are you
acknowledging the bigger story in your prayer life?

In light of Scripture and based on your responses,
quiet yourself before the Lord and spend a few moments in prayer.

CREDIT WHERE CREDIT IS DUE

Read Judges 5:12-31.

In verses 14-18 Deborah turned her attention to the people. She spoke of individual tribes and called them by name, being clear about those who showed up for the battle and those who didn't. The tribes of Epraim, Benjamin, Issachar, Zebulun, and Naphtali joined the fight and risked their lives on the battlefield. But Reuben, Gilead, Dan, and Asher stayed home. To their shame, they didn't act.

The victory didn't belong to the tribes who came, and the tribes who didn't come wouldn't be left out of the blessing. When the people of God prevail, it's because He's working for them. Those who choose to sit on the sidelines miss joining His mighty work. The people don't own the mission. We join a mission that's bigger than ourselves.

This idea was beautifully expressed when Deborah painted a word picture of the battle itself, with all creation heeding the word of the Lord (see vv. 20-22). Yahweh called, the world answered, and the Israelites had a front-row seat. Those who came got to see victory delivered into their hands.

Deborah's humility shone through in her prayer when she highlighted the courageous act of Jael (see vv. 24-27). When she had told Barak that honor would go to a woman, at first glance the reader might think Deborah would claim that honor for herself. But she was foreshadowing the act of a woman in a tent who would dispatch the enemy with no fanfare. In her moment before the Lord and before Israel, Deborah offered a blessing to someone else. Deborah's leadership was shining through, but she didn't hold on to honor. She bestowed honor.

After telling the details of Sisera's demise, Deborah closed her song of praise by appealing to God's loyalty (see v. 31). Earlier she had seen that God would take care of His people in this crisis, and now she saw that He would take care of them in crises to come. This is the story of redemption. Enemies of the Lord will perish. His children will rise like the sun.

Deborah was a judge for her people. She led with wisdom and truth. She helped lead an army in battle. She honored a courageous woman. But she didn't claim victory for herself. She knew that victory belonged to the Lord.

PRAYER

Enter this time with your Bible and your heart open.
Based on the truths of Scripture, answer the following
questions and let them lead you to a time of prayer.

PRAISE

Reread Judges 5 and express Deborah's prayer of praise in your own words. Personalize the prayer by applying it to a season in your life when the Lord won a great victory.

REPENT

Who gets the credit in your victories? Do you struggle with wanting it for yourself? Confess that the Lord is your sole source of victory and blessing.

APPLY

Humility can be developed through deferential prayers. How does the way you pray discourage you from claiming victory for yourself?

YIELD

Praying for humility is difficult because God might teach it to us by placing us in humbling situations. What steps can you take to cultivate humility?

In light of Scripture and based on your responses,
quiet yourself before the Lord and spend a few moments in prayer.

LESSONS FROM DEBORAH'S PRAYER

Reread Judges 4–5.

The best way to know a person's heart and disposition is to hear his or her prayers. We see Deborah's heart through her song of praise.

Don't run from God's call. When Deborah learned of God's command to Barak, she immediately summoned Barak. She herself was receiving a call, and she owned her role as a mother in Israel.

Don't fear action. Deborah acted. Her fortitude didn't spring from a sense of personal bravado but from the knowledge that the Lord had heard the cries of His people. Her courage came from the belief that deliverance would come from an outside source. Her faith led to action.

Encourage others. Deborah didn't dismiss Barak when he was afraid. She challenged him. She agreed to go with him. She consistently reminded him that victory was certain. When she sang her song of praise, she sang it with Barak.

Point people back to the mission. Deborah always knew God would save His people. She walked with Barak to a victory that was certain and would include their active participation. She showed the tribes what they had experienced, as well as what some of them had missed.

Give honor to the Lord. Deborah knew before the army went out that the Lord had gone before it. When the battle was over, her response to victory was to acknowledge God's sovereign hand in the care of His people. She celebrated the actions of the people as a reason to praise their Redeemer.

We see someone's heart through their prayers. Often we only get to hear them asking for help in a crisis. Cries of desperation can certainly give us a picture of the leader's soul and can show us how to depend on the Lord in the darkest moments. But Deborah allowed us to hear her voice after the crisis was over, and her humility and dependence on God were just as real.

True character comes through in moments of crisis, but the character that remains after victory is equally telling. When we cry out to the Lord and He answers, let's be people who see Him and praise Him for what He has done. Genuine leadership gives honor to God.

PRAYER

Enter this time with your Bible and your heart open.
Based on the truths of Scripture, answer the following
questions and let them lead you to a time of prayer.

PRAISE

Evaluate your life against the measuring stick of Deborah's prayer, praise, and worship. Where are these activities present in your life?

REPENT

Have you missed opportunities to show God glory for what He has done? How have you failed to draw attention to God's goodness toward your church?

APPLY

Make sure you're giving thanks to God in your life. Then work in positive, constructive ways to live with thanksgiving.

YIELD

Deborah and Barak stood shoulder to shoulder at a pivotal time in the life of God's people. One stepped back, while the other moved ahead. One trusted his companion, while the other trusted her God. Are you prepared to trust the Lord and take the first step, confident that the Lord you serve will provide the necessary resources? Following the victory, will you have a humble heart and express honor to His name?

In light of Scripture and based on your responses,
quiet yourself before the Lord and spend a few moments in prayer.

Welcome to group session 4 of *Praying at the Crossroads.*

Use the following questions to begin the session.

Have you ever prayed so long and hard for something that you wondered whether God actually heard you?

How many sincere truth seekers have read, studied, and emulated the prayers of faithful Hannah? Her deeply personal entreaties to the Lord inspire and instruct us in prayer that's humble, honest, hopeful, habitual, and hugely thankful. Many believers find themselves among minions of prayer-warrior wannabes hungry for rich communion with our Father like Hannah's. Month after month, year after year Hannah waited for God's blessing of a child, praying from the depths of her soul.

Hannah's prayer was honed in personal relationship. Hannah recognized the good blessing of children as the Lord's provision. The reality of her own barrenness became painful fodder for taunts from less-loved but ever-pregnant Peninnah. Every jeer, every snide remark increased Hannah's longing ache in her perpetual disappointment.

Hannah repeatedly came to the Lord with the same petition, signaling confidence that He heard even if she couldn't see His divine yes in response. Such regular, persistent communication indicates a growing relationship with God.

How does a personal, intimate relationship with God affect a person's prayer life?

Use these statements to follow along as you watch video session 4.

God had a mighty plan in store for Samuel.

We found, in that experience, the grace of God, not what we wanted.

God does hear, and God does answer. Very often His answer is a magnificent yes.

Sometimes His answer is "Wait for the Lord."

There are times when God, as our all-wise, all-loving Father, has to say no.

Video sessions available at lifeway.com/prayingatthecrossroads or with a subscription to smallgroup.com

DISCUSS

Use the following questions to discuss the video teaching.

Read I Samuel 1.

How would you describe Hannah's life circumstance?

Do thoughts of fairness and unfairness come to mind as you read Hannah's story?

Hannah's barrenness poured out in fervent prayer for a baby, while her husband's rival wife, Peninnah, year after year bore him both sons and daughters. Elkanah's attempt at comfort is recorded in verse 8: "Hannah, why are you crying? ... Am I not better to you than ten sons?" Marriage is the primary relationship in a family, but is this a husband's appropriate response to his wife's grief?

Even as we embrace God's sovereignty, how could a person's prayer life be affected by long years of waiting? Consider both pros and cons.

How can daily, habitual prayer influence a Christian's spontaneous prayers?

Hannah's prayer was directed to the One she knew was there, who heard, cared, and was able to meet her need. As Hannah pleaded with the Lord, she simultaneously offered Him the dearest request of her heart. If God would give Hannah a son, she would relinquish her son back the Lord in service to Him. Hannah recognized that God alone could bring life where there was none.

Were Hannah's words in verse 11 a bargain with God or a faith element of her prayer?

Verses 20 and 27 herald God's gift to Hannah—her baby boy, Samuel. The name Samuel means "name of God" or "one who comes from God." Hannah's words in verse 27 proclaim her joyful recognition that the little boy she now held was God's direct answer to her long-offered prayers.

Read I Samuel 1:20,27. When God obviously intervenes to answer your prayer, what's your typical response?

Read verses 27-28. What do these verses indicate about Hannah's example and testimony of prayer before her son?

First Samuel 2:1-10 records Hannah's song of thanksgiving for the birth of Samuel. An often repeated theme in Scripture is God's faithful care for people who are weak and helpless. He responds with power and might to strengthen those who humbly trust in Him.

Read James 4:6. How do you see this principle illuminated in Hannah's prayer of thanks?

God magnificently answered Hannah's prayer for a baby in the gift of her son, Samuel. God always hears and answers our prayers. However, we must also recognize that sometimes God's answer to our honest, heartfelt prayer is no. In those moments God is still God, and He's still good. We entrust our hearts and our souls to God, trusting His best will for us. Although we may not receive the answer we request, God always answers our prayers.

How should God's child respond when His answer as a loving Father is no?

GROUP PRAYER

Use the following PRAY framework to pray together as a group.

In light of what we've studied today, pray together as a group, using the following prompts to guide your experience together. You'll repeat this exercise at the end of each day's personal study. Use the biblical prayer we studied to guide your own. Read each prompt aloud and encourage group members to lift up prayers based on these prompts silently or aloud, depending on their comfort level.

PRAISE *God for who He is and what He has done.*

Even when life is hard, we're blessed. Hannah's husband provided for her and annually took her to the temple. What are you thankful for?

REPENT *of unconfessed sins and accept Christ's forgiveness.*

Each of us is a sinner. Hannah surely envied Peninnah and may have felt tempted to retaliate. Ask the Lord to reveal sin in your heart. Then confess it and ask for His forgiveness.

APPLY *the truths you've learned by committing to action.*

Are you willing to boldly ask the Lord for your heart's desire, then wait for Him to respond according to His perfect will and timing? Consider Hannah's example: "I've been pouring out my heart before the LORD" (1 Sam. 1:15).

YIELD *your life to God's will and kind providence.*

Hannah entrusted to God's hands her life and that of the baby for whom she hoped. Let the prayer of Jesus be our own: "Your will be done" (Matt. 26:42).

Close by praying for specific requests that arose during the session.

HUMBLE PRAYER

Read 1 Samuel 1:11.

Notice the way Hannah referred to herself when speaking to the Lord: "your servant." Hannah and the Lord enjoyed a genuine, vital relationship, to be sure, but not as peers. God was the LORD of Armies. Hannah was His servant. She would bow in humble submission to His will while maintaining an open stream of praise and petition.

A common misconception in our culture assumes that God is somehow our equal, a kind of cloud-wrapped, divine great-uncle sort, with whom an earthling can banter, obligate, demand, or even demean at will. Such presumption is terrifying. Holy God, LORD of Armies, supreme holder of all power and authority, bends down from His magnificence to hear lowly humans (see Ps. 116:1-2).Hannah took her "anguish and resentment" (1 Sam. 1:16) to the only One who could bring her true peace.

Many people with whom I pray have had no previous relationship with God and therefore have never talked with Him in prayer. Their first steps toward God never fail to bless my heart. After prayer in one initial visit, the patient said, "Wow. It sounded as if you were really talking to somebody." He later asked if he could personally know God too and that day humbly opened his heart to God in prayer.

Another patient, an elderly woman, became a friend through daily visits. She shared her life experiences and current condition with transparency, always requesting prayer but often reminding me that she hadn't attended church for many years. One day as I prayed with her, she interrupted "Lord, You know I haven't been to church in a long time, and now I'm old and sick. But if You still want me, You can have whatever I've got left. Well, I love Ya. Bye."

Through humble, earnest prayer she came to the Savior, trusting Him for forgiveness and peace. I'm sure He heard and cherished her childlike prayer.

When called to the bedside of a very sick patient, I sometimes ask, "What are you thankful for?" or "Do you have any regrets?" We thank God for expressed blessings. If tears of humble confession follow, the person can take those to God in prayer and ask for His forgiveness. Tender prayers of confession and divine forgiveness bring peace and promise to a troubled soul, often restoring human relationships as well. Remember, God "gives grace to the humble" (Jas. 4:6).

PRAYER

Enter this time with your Bible and your heart open.
Based on the truths of Scripture, answer the following
questions and let them lead you to a time of prayer.

PRAISE

Praise God for His willingness to listen to your prayer anytime, anywhere.

REPENT

Repent of any ugly pride lurking in your heart. Pride is the sin God detests most.

APPLY

Apply Hannah's humble servant spirit, asking God to make it your own.

YIELD

Yield all of the hours of your day to God's will and kind providence.

In light of Scripture and based on your responses,
quiet yourself before the Lord and spend a few moments in prayer.

HONEST PRAYER

Read 1 Samuel 1:11.

As a child in Sunday School, I learned to pray "for the sick and afflicted, for missionaries on the foreign fields, and for all of those for whom it's our duty to pray." Verbatim. Covered all of the bases.

Hannah, however, approached the Lord in the temple with her specific need, asking Him simply and clearly to meet that need. She did more than ask. She "wept with many tears" (v. 10). She "pleaded" (v. 11). She even made a vow to the Lord if He would fulfill her request (see v. 11). Her prayer was so silently fervent, lips moving without verbal sound, "Eli thought she was drunk" and scolded her (v. 14). But Hannah responded, "No, my lord. … I've been pouring out my heart before the LORD" (v. 15).

Unaffected by the possibility that other people would observe her or misjudge her character, Hannah poured out her heart to the Lord. All her attention was on the LORD of Armies, who heard her heartfelt cry. "The prayer of a righteous person is very powerful in its effect" (Jas. 5:16).

Did God already know the desire of Hannah's heart? Absolutely. He had heard her prayers more times than she could count; He knew and remembered each one. God never tires of hearing the sincere petitions of His children. Hannah's repeated plea never grew stale, and neither do ours.

Yesterday I found a note requesting prayer. It included the date and time in my own handwriting, but it had no name or explanation, no clue of the person's identity who had asked for prayer. I mentally pictured a needy soul requesting the chaplain to pray before surgery, but I couldn't recall the particular person.

I fervently asked God to bring to memory the person behind that note. Later in the day when a nurse mentioned a certain clinical procedure, a mental lightbulb flashed. Aha! It was the same procedure this certain person would have on this particular date.

Did the Lord drop that little nugget like manna from heaven? James 1:17 says, "Every good and perfect gift is from above, coming down from the Father of lights," so I heartily whispered, "Thank You, Lord."

Did the Father remove all forgetfulness and restore my young mind? No. Will I keep my word when the appointed day comes? It's now recorded on the calendar. God heard Hannah, and He hears us.

PRAYER

Enter this time with your Bible and your heart open.
Based on the truths of Scripture, answer the following
questions and let them lead you to a time of prayer.

PRAISE

Praise and worship God by completing the sentence "You are …"

REPENT

Repent with sincere, specific confession of any act, motive, or attitude that was or is disobedient to God. Ask for His forgiveness. Then accept His fresh washing of your heart.

APPLY

Apply God's invitation by bringing your requests to Him.

YIELD

Yield your time, energy, and resources to God's use, praying, "Whatever, Lord."

In light of Scripture and based on your responses,
quiet yourself before the Lord and spend a few moments in prayer.

HOPEFUL PRAYER

Read 1 Samuel 1:11.

Hannah's prayer was hopeful. As she prayed for a son, an action plan hatched for the time of her heart desire's fulfillment. She would "give him to the LORD all the days of his life."

Paul's beautiful treatise on divine love in 1 Corinthians 13 concludes with a list of three essentials—faith, hope, and love (v. 13). Faith is foundational for salvation, but Paul said love is the greatest of all, even above faith. What about hope?

Standing between two powerhouses, faith and love, hope might seem the underdog, certainly less emphasized in many doctrinal discussions. Yet Hebrews 6:19 describes hope as "an anchor for the soul." True, biblical, God-given hope. Eternal hope in God, who has drawn us to Himself before forming our eyelashes or our first breath, who hears our prayers. Hope that gets us up in the morning, propels us through our days, and gives us evening rest. This is no fingers-crossed "I hope so" but the assurance of God's full attention to our needs as we come to Him in childlike faith. I cling to it, and so did Hannah.

Hannah would leave her beloved little boy with a doddering old priest and his two repulsive sons, rowdies who were notorious for practicing immorality in the temple where they "served" with utter irreverence and who ended up losing the ark of the covenant in battle.

Would you leave your innocent child in the company of such hoodlums? But Hannah's faith in God, who was great enough to give her a son, included His net of protection around that asked-for little boy, even in the most precarious situation. Her prayer was rooted in and fueled by hope.

Hannah left the temple with gracious respect for Eli and a peaceful, hopeful spirit: "Hannah went on her way; she ate and no longer looked despondent" (1 Sam. 1:18).

PRAYER

Enter this time with your Bible and your heart open.
Based on the truths of Scripture, answer the following
questions and let them lead you to a time of prayer.

PRAISE

Praise God for His Word to you, the Bible, your source of wisdom, comfort, joy, and hope.

REPENT

Repent of unbelief. Is anything too hard for God? Confess your lack of faith.

APPLY

Ask God for one request that seems unlikely or even impossible.

YIELD

Yield the outcome to God's perfect will and timing. Be willing to wait.

In light of Scripture and based on your responses,
quiet yourself before the Lord and spend a few moments in prayer.

HABITUAL PRAYER

> **Read 1 Samuel 1:19.**

The next morning divine peace remained evident as Hannah and her husband began the day with reverent worship. From this reference we picture morning prayer as Hannah's daily habit. Elkanah may have joined her in prayer daily. We know for sure that extra time was intentionally allotted this particular morning. They set the alarm early for prayer before the long journey home.

Proverbs 15:8 says God delights in our prayers. As a grandmother, I expectantly bend forward, calling "Come to Grannie!" in delight when my smiling grandbabies reach into a joyful hug. How much more does Father God's heart warm when we come to Him as Hannah did.

God honored Hannah's faithful, sincere prayers. She firmly believed she was able to have a son because she "requested him from the LORD" (1 Sam. 1:20). The holy LORD of Armies heard Hannah's prayer and granted her request. She not only became pregnant but also delivered a healthy son. She got exactly what she asked for. Every pray-er hopes to ask and receive, to see the fulfillment of the heart's expressed desire. Hannah asked God for a son, and she later held a healthy baby.

If you've ever struggled with whether God hears your prayers because they seem unanswered, you're not alone. Yes, Hannah received her first baby, Samuel, and more (see 2:21). But Hannah's name is never mentioned again in Scripture, leaving us unaware of her other prayer experiences.

I too asked God for a baby. God answered "above and beyond all that we ask or think" (Eph. 3:20). Triplets, premature but healthy. How we praised Him!

Life was good. Our three little Texans grew, thrived, and excelled. When they were thirteen, our family was preparing for a move to Missouri. Shrieking fire alarms startled us awake in predawn darkness to the stench of smoke. Our house was ablaze, but we escaped. We thanked God that although the house burned, our home was intact. He was good and faithful.

A few months later, the rebuilding project almost complete, we joyfully prepared to join my husband in Saint Louis. In the transition a routine medical exam revealed that Anna had advanced leukemia. Anna seemed healthy and energetic, a genuine joy to everyone who knew her. How could this be? We took another enormous burden to the Lord in prayer.

PRAYER

Enter this time with your Bible and your heart open.
Based on the truths of Scripture, answer the following
questions and let them lead you to a time of prayer.

PRAISE

Praise God for His infinite mercy, His lovingkindness that's new every morning (see Lam. 3:23).

REPENT

Repent for running to God eagerly in emergencies but grudgingly in early mornings.

APPLY

Apply your heart to God's wisdom daily, storing His truth in your heart for the Holy Spirit to apply in times of need. If a verse comes to mind, pray it to Him.

YIELD

Yield all of your material things, financial assets, relationships, and human ambitions to God's good will and purpose.

In light of Scripture and based on your responses,
quiet yourself before the Lord and spend a few moments in prayer.

HUGELY THANKFUL PRAYER

Read 1 Samuel 2:1-2.

Knowing God had answered her plea for a baby, Hannah thanked Him profusely.

When my children were born, I made two promises to God if He would let our tiny babies survive: I wouldn't complain about taking care of them, and I would remember to say, "Thank You" for them.

God heard and answered Hannah's prayer by giving her Samuel. He also heard and answered my prayers by giving us Joshua, Jonathan, and Anna Joy. Surely God would again answer by healing Anna of leukemia.

Fifteen months of chemotherapy, radiation, a stem-cell transplant from brother Joshua, and amazing twists and rebounds tested every fiber of our endurance. Many nurses, technicians, and patients in the hospital saw and experienced the fragrance of Christ through sweet Anna. One who came to saving faith was her brilliant oncologist. In a wheelchair on oxygen, Anna watched her daddy baptize Dr. Rob Hanson on a bright Sunday morning.

We continued to trust, knowing with certainty Anna and the rest of us were held in God's loving, faithful hands. We asked for her healing and prayed that His will would be done.

Saturday evening, August 17, 1996, I leaned over darling, cherished Anna Joy and whispered the hardest words to her: "If Jesus comes tonight and asks you to go with Him, turn loose of Mama's hand and take His hand. It's the right thing to do." Sunday morning the Savior gently, tenderly carried Anna from earth to heaven.

In the years since that day I've often pondered God's plan. Did He hear my prayers for a baby? Yes. Did He also hear my prayers and those of many other believers for Anna's healing? Yes, just as surely.

I've come to understand that God always hears and always answers our prayers. Sometimes, as in Hannah's case and mine, He answers yes, and great rejoicing ensues. Other times He gently but firmly answers, "Dear child, I must say no."

God is our faithful, loving Father. He tenderly responds as the sovereign designer of the end from the beginning (see Isa. 46:10), who has numbered all of our days before there's yet one of them (see Ps. 139:16), whose plan is perfect. I trusted Him in barrenness and learned to trust Him even more in the depths of sorrow and loss. Blessed be our Lord and Father, who daily bears our burdens, who hears and answers every prayer.

PRAYER

Enter this time with your Bible and your heart open.
Based on the truths of Scripture, answer the following
questions and let them lead you to a time of prayer.

PRAISE

Praise God for all of His wonderful works, from creation to the cross; from the cross to the resurrection; from the resurrection to His saving, sustaining grace in your life.

REPENT

Turn away from desires and pursuits that aren't God's will for you. Tell Him you're sorry and ask Him to forgive you. Then sense the peace of His forgiveness.

APPLY

Thank God for every blessing the Holy Spirit brings to mind. Thank Him for carrying you through painful times. Thank Him for His promise to someday wipe away all of your tears.

YIELD

Yield to God's plan, knowing He loved you first and best. He's got you, dear child. Cling to Him. Rest in Him. Depend on Him. Trust Him now and forever.

In light of Scripture and based on your responses,
quiet yourself before the Lord and spend a few moments in prayer.

WEEK 5

The Prayer of Solomon

Welcome to group session 5 of *Praying at the Crossroads.*

Use the following questions to begin the session.

When was the most recent time you faced a difficult decision? How did you respond? What strategy did you use to reach a conclusion?

Have you ever waited too late or rushed too early and missed the right choice? What should you have done differently?

All of us are faced with decisions at some point in time. We daily make decisions of different types and levels of importance. Solomon was a national leader who made long-term choices and responded to them. Not all of them were perfect, and not all of them pleased God. But in 1 Kings 8 Solomon made decisions that helped turn the nation of Israel back in a direction that would not only prove pleasing to God but would also have long-term implications beyond their days, even into the New Testament.

The people of God were at a historical and spiritual crossroads. They sat at an intersection of history, experience, and relationship with God. After years the hopes and dreams of King David were to be fulfilled by his son Solomon. With much planning, praying, and dreaming, the temple had been carefully constructed according to a specific design. It was finally complete. A permanent place to worship God had been built. A place for people to meet with God had been created.

As soon as the ark was brought into the holy of holies, the shekinah glory of God descended on the temple.

Solomon declared the glory of the Lord and recognized who God is.

Solomon recognized God's love, grace, justice, and holiness.

Solomon acknowledged that God is the Lord of all the nations and that the nations would come to the temple to worship, pray, and praise Him there.

Israel had a mission to be a light and a model for all the nations to see.

Solomon finished his prayer by leading the people in worship.

Application from Solomon's Prayer

1. Not only how we celebrate our past but also who we need to be next

2. Knowing God—understanding who He is, His characteristics, His attributes, and His blessings

Hang on because God has a plan, and if you stick with Him, you're going to have victory.

DISCUSS

Use the following questions to discuss the video teaching.

Read 1 Kings 8:22-53.

What's the connection between God's faithfulness and His sovereignty? How do we see both in Solomon's prayer?

Although God wants us to pray for our needs, how could our prayer lives be enriched by going beyond needs-based requests?

Often the prayers we find in the Bible are very different from our own. Prayers in the Bible proclaim to God who He is and praise Him for His nature and character. Scripture reminds us to thank God for the grace and blessings He has shown us. The grace we receive from God should lead to prayers in which we humbly and brokenly agree with Him about our sin and seek His forgiveness.

On the video Dr. Ewart said the temple provides evidence that God wants us to come near Him and to know Him. How would it change the way you pray if you approached God knowing that He's willing to hear you?

Though our sins are forgiven in Christ, why should we continue to confess them to God ? How does this practice help us fight against sin?

Solomon prayed for the people's forgiveness. He didn't say *if* they sinned but *when* they sinned. All people, even redeemed ones, are prone to sin. Our sin isn't hidden from God, who's the ultimate judge. Whether the sin was a part of their personal relationships or a national sin, Solomon asked God to hear and forgive. Taking our sins to God and confessing them thus removes the guilt and shame we feel and allows us to receive the forgiveness that He freely gives to all who ask.

Reread verse 41. God isn't just the national God of Israel. He's the only living God. When Solomon prayed for the foreigner, who could that be in our context? How should this request shape our prayers?

Solomon prayed that the temple would reach and teach the nations about the true God, not separate them from Him. The temple was the sign that the God of Israel dwelled among His people and invited the nations to know Him. He prayed that they would come there to see and experience Him. He asked that they would be allowed to pray to God and that He would listen to their prayers. The law and the temple were to illustrate a walk with Yahweh. The temple was to be an invitation for people to come and experience intimacy with the one true God.

> *Solomon prayed for victory, protection, justice, and security. When was the most recent time you prayed for these concerns?*

Hopefully, you're seeing through this study that God is willing to hear our prayers in a variety of circumstances. No concern surprises or frustrates God. He longs to hear from us and give us the opportunity to speak and commune with Him. The temple embodies that truth.

> *What's the most recent answer to prayer you received from God? Share and celebrate with the group.*

When we seek to follow God's will, we can pray for victory. We can also pray for security and provision. Solomon prayed for the continual fulfillment of God's promise to His people. The nation of Israel was under His care and authority.

> *How would believers' influence on our culture change if we were seen as people who truly celebrate God's victory and goodness?*

GROUP PRAYER

Use the following PRAY framework to pray together as a group.

In light of what we've studied today, pray together as a group, using the following prompts to guide your experience together. You'll repeat this exercise at the end of each day's personal study. Use the biblical prayer we studied to guide your own. Read each prompt aloud and encourage group members to lift up prayers based on these prompts silently or aloud, depending on their comfort level.

PRAISE God for who He is and what He has done.

As God was faithful to Israel in building His temple and dwelling among them, He's faithful to us today. Praise God for always being with you in Christ, who has made you His temple through the indwelling presence of the Holy Spirit (see 1 Cor. 6:19).

REPENT of unconfessed sins and accept Christ's forgiveness.

Solomon recognized national and personal sins in the lives of the people who would worship at God's temple. Confess the ways you've sinned individually and collectively as the church.

APPLY the truths you've learned by committing to action.

The Lord designed the temple to be a beacon to the nations. This is precisely what He has called us to be in the Great Commission (see Matt. 28:18-20). Pray that God will give you an opportunity to share the gospel with a "foreigner."

YIELD your life to God's will and kind providence.

God isn't just the national God of Israel but the Lord of all the earth, who's committed to taking His glory to the ends of the earth. Yield your life to Him, expressing your willingness to listen when He calls and to go where He leads.

Close by praying for specific requests that arose during the session.

PREPARATION FOR PRAYER

Read 1 Kings 8:1–11.

Before the temple could be officially dedicated and ongoing sacrificial offerings could be made, the final, most important piece had to be brought to its resting place. In these verses the ark of the covenant was brought to the temple, symbolizing the indwelling of the very presence of God and a welcome to His house. The Jewish people sought to usher Him in with the greatest care and honor.

This grand event took place, very appropriately, during the Feast of Booths. The last of the yearly feasts was a time of harvest that celebrated the end of the wilderness wandering and God's bringing His people to the land of promise. The dedication of this new dwelling place for worship and sacrifice was a climactic expression of that deliverance and fulfillment. King Solomon and the people gathered before the ark, sacrificing animals in huge numbers, probably in the outer temple court as the ark arrived there. The very presence of God was welcomed, and the entry was paved with sacrifice and offering.

Imagine the drama and pageantry, with the priests leading the procession of the ark. We know from 2 Chronicles that levitical musicians were also engaged to play music. The sights and sounds would have awed the people, filling their hearts with joy and praise. What a high and holy moment for them!

When the ark reached its final resting place, the inner room became the holy of holies. The glory of God entered the temple, His presence demonstrating His authenticity and divine approval. The glory of the Lord is like a consuming fire, and no one can stand in it presence. The priests couldn't remain because His presence was simply too much for them. They had to move out of the way and allow God to be displayed. What an awesome event to behold!

According to Hebrews 4, we now have an opportunity to approach God's throne of grace with confidence (see v. 16) because Jesus made a final, complete sacrifice for us The idea of confidence in that passage means "with complete honesty and without fear." God wants us to come to Him with an open heart. We can hide nothing from Him. We are now also the temple of the Holy Spirit (see 1 Cor. 6:19).

PRAYER

Enter this time with your Bible and your heart open.
Based on the truths of Scripture, answer the following
questions and let them lead you to a time of prayer.

PRAISE

Do people see God's glory and presence in your daily life? Are you praising God and making the sacrifices He deserves?

REPENT

For the priest to participate in the celebration, he had to be ceremonially clean. What sin in your life is keeping you from being able to serve God fully?

APPLY

How careful and consistent are you to reflect the presence of God in your daily life? How are you specifically doing that? Do other people see His presence in your attitudes and actions?

YIELD

These verses in 1 Kings 8 describe the preparations for the celebration of the temple. God is constantly preparing us to do His work. How are you cooperating with God in this preparation?

In light of Scripture and based on your responses,
quiet yourself before the Lord and spend a few moments in prayer.

GOD'S PROMISES AND FAITHFULNESS

Read 1 Kings 8:12–21.

This passage is the preamble to the main prayer Solomon offered in verses 22-53. It's the prayer before the prayer. The content of this preprayer is the faithfulness of God and His goodness toward those who love Him. Here the king stepped up to address the people and God. His desire was that both would hear as He interceded and mediated on their behalf. His heart surely swelled as he remembered the songs of prayer and praise written by and for his father.

Solomon began by expressing thanksgiving to God for always keeping His promises. The only appropriate response for the king was one of complete appreciation and wonder. God had just honored the nation with His overwhelming presence. They must and should honor Him in return.

In verses 14-21 Solomon sought to express that honor as He blessed the people and the Lord. He recalled the promises God made to David and his father's desire to build the temple himself. The king declared the fulfillment of that promise and dream.

This moment marks an end. The people were truly home. A kingdom was established that stretched farther than ever before or would ever again. Its wealth was never surpassed in its history. Its power was to be feared. The covenant with David was coming true.

This event truly celebrated the finale of the exodus to the promised land and of God's promises for the people's future. This moment also marked a new beginning. Crossroads moments do that. It was time for the people to decide who they would be next. Would they truly be the people of Yahweh? Would they be a light to the other nations? Would they surrender and obey Jehovah?

Each person has this choice each day. Will we honor God? Will we obey? We don't obey to earn God's favor; this has already been given to us in Christ. We obey because God loves us and is always good and faithful toward us. God's past actions indicate that He has no intention of ever being unfaithful. As His followers, we reflect on His faithfulness and commit each day to declare His promises to ourselves and to those with whom we come into contact who need to know God.

PRAYER

Enter this time with your Bible and your heart open.
Based on the truths of Scripture, answer the following
questions and let them lead you to a time of prayer.

PRAISE

Solomon thanked God for His faithfulness and deliverance (see vv. 15-16),
as well as His promises to David (see v. 20). How has God been faithful
to you and your family this week or this day?

REPENT

When God shows Himself in your life, how do you respond? When He answers
a prayer, proves His faithfulness, blesses you, and displays His power and love,
what do you do? When have you spurned or underappreciated God's grace?

APPLY

What does it look like to live with complete appreciation for God? How could
your interaction with others be different if you savored God above all else?

YIELD

In light of God's faithfulness, Israel was faced with the choice to honor God.
We have this same choice every day. How will you honor God today?

In light of Scripture and based on your responses,
quiet yourself before the Lord and spend a few moments in prayer.

KNOWING GOD THROUGH PRAYER

Read 1 Kings 8:22-53

On this new day King Solomon stood before the whole assembly on a bronze platform and prayed as a representative of and mediator for his people. He prayed for God's people and others to know who God was, what He had done, and what He would do.

Know God's faithfulness and sovereignty (see vv. 22-26). Recognizing God's superiority means acknowledging there's no god like Him. God is completely unique and faithful, merciful and gracious. Solomon asked for his family line to continue and to be blessed. He was depending on God's faithfulness for this and all else to be accomplished.

Know God's greatness and willingness to hear our prayers (see vv. 27-29). God is too great for a physical building to contain, yet He's willing to listen to our prayers. Even though His full presence would destroy us, He reveals Himself to us and allows us to know Him personally.

Know God's justice, forgiveness, and mercy (see vv. 30-40). Anticipating that the nation would sin, Solomon prayed for the people's forgiveness. Times of national, corporate sin would come. The king prayed that the people would learn lessons from their failures, repent of their sins, and avoid those mistakes in the future. Solomon also prayed about personal sin. Like corporate sin, individual sin requires personal repentance. Each person must confess and seek forgiveness.

Know God even as foreigners (see vv. 41-43). Solomon went on to pray for people who weren't part of the Hebrew people and didn't yet know God. He prayed for the nations to come to know Him.

Know God's victory, protection, justice, and security (see vv. 44-53). The king also prayed for the people of Israel who were far away with no access to the temple, such as soldiers in the army. He wanted no one to be left out.

When we're seeking to follow God's will, we can pray for victory. We can also pray for security and provision. Solomon prayed for the continual fulfillment of God's promise to His people, believing they were under His care and authority. The people of Israel needed hope for the present and the future. This prayer would serve as a reminder and a challenge. Solomon prayed that the nation would be a memorial for God to show the world.

PRAYER

Enter this time with your Bible and your heart open.
Based on the truths of Scripture, answer the following
questions and let them lead you to a time of prayer.

PRAISE

How much of your prayer life consists of simply asking God for things you desire? Begin your prayer today by praising Him for His nature and character, as Solomon did in verses 22-26.

REPENT

Cry out to the Lord about our national or corporate sin (see vv. 33-34) and your personal sin (see vv. 38-40).

APPLY

To teach their people to pray well, leaders must pray well themselves. Focus on your times of personal prayer and on the requests you're asking of God. Focus on times of public prayer and truly think about what you're saying and teaching as you pray.

YIELD

Our prayer lives can be reflections and expressions of our walk with God when we broaden and deepen our hearts and minds. Slow down and take time to pray well.

In light of Scripture and based on your responses,
quiet yourself before the Lord and spend a few moments in prayer.

BLESSING AND BENEDICTION

Read 1 Kings 8:54–61.

Having bowed in humility before the Lord at His altar, Solomon rose after his dramatic prayer. Again he glorified God for His faithfulness. He began his prayer with praise and ended it with praise to God, recognizing His rich, abundant blessing.

It's from the realization and affirmation of God's faithfulness to Israel that Solomon also pleaded for the people to be as faithful to God as He had been to them. He prayed that their hearts would turn to God and that they would always know the importance of His presence in their lives. Living before the face of God changes the way we relate to the world around us. Active faithfulness gives a powerful, unshakable sense of peace.

A key word Solomon used was *rest* (v. 56). Rest comes from a faithful, obedient life. Rest doesn't mean that our lives will be easy but rather that no matter what we encounter, God grants us peace through His Spirit. God is always with us. He doesn't do what people do and abandon us at the first sign of hardship. The confidence that emanates from His presence gives us peace.

This is a prayer of peace and presence. This is a prayer of relationship and fellowship. This is a prayer of fulfillment. Solomon prayed that God would sustain and keep the people as they kept His words, law, and covenant. The temple service would be a major component of that promise.

The Lord is the only true God. All other gods are empty idols. The recognition of God's utter uniqueness in verse 60 is in effect a call to worship Him. Solomon felt comfortable presenting his needs to God because he realized He's the only One who can meet those needs. He alone is perfect in power and ability, so we go to Him in prayer.

Solomon wanted his words to continuously be before the Lord. He never wanted God to forget him and his people. He also challenged the people never to forget God, to keep His law, and to give Him their whole hearts.

PRAYER

*Enter this time with your Bible and your heart open.
Based on the truths of Scripture, answer the following
questions and let them lead you to a time of prayer.*

PRAISE

Do your prayers lead to action? Commitment? Renewal? Why or why not?
What's one action, commitment, or renewal you need to make today?
How is taking action a form of worship?

REPENT

What actions has God urged you to take that you haven't taken?

APPLY

The work God has done should lead us to observe the rest He has given
us (see v. 56). When will you prioritize rest?

YIELD

How will you "be wholeheartedly devoted to the LORD our God to walk
in his statutes and to keep his commands" (v. 61)?

*In light of Scripture and based on your responses,
quiet yourself before the Lord and spend a few moments in prayer.*

SACRIFICES OF WORSHIP

Read 1 Kings 8:62–66.

We might tend to skip passages of Scripture that describe sacrifices. But we must remember that God inspired every sacrifice, both the action and the recording of it. God gave us a record of this sacrifice to read and celebrate.

The sacrifices offered in response to Solomon's prayer were expressions of worship. And the celebration continued for two weeks. Talk about a revival! Thousands of animals were sacrificed. Sacrifice and praise dedicated the new sanctuary—housewarming gifts for the King of kings.

How the blood flowed! It was shed to honor God and to cleanse the people. The sheer number of sacrifices and offerings meant the whole courtyard had to be consecrated and used. Imagine such a sight. How meager some of our sacrifices for the Lord must seem. Solomon and Israel remembered the importance of giving of themselves and their treasure to worship the God of heaven. The people stayed at the temple and worshiped for fourteen days. All went home thankful, filled with gladness and joy over what God had done.

This experience unified the people for a time. Renewed and challenged, they recommitted themselves to serve their Lord and to be His people. Passionate worship drives thankful, unified, and sacrificial living.

Questions remain for you. Is your life being shaped by decisions of dedication? How is your devotion to the Lord and to others growing daily? Jesus commanded us to love God and others (see Matt. 22:37-39). These two relationships define everything about us as Christians. They both come from a heart that has been transformed by the gospel and given to the Lord in recognition of all He has done for us. Ultimately, His sacrifice for us leads to our sacrifice for Him. Sacrifice is fueled by decisions of dedication.

PRAYER

Enter this time with your Bible and your heart open.
Based on the truths of Scripture, answer the following
questions and let them lead you to a time of prayer.

PRAISE

The product of prayer is worship. How is the act of prayer producing praise in you?

REPENT

Sacrifices should cost you something. What "sacrifices" have you offered the Lord that actually cost you nothing?

APPLY

What sacrifices could you make to deepen your commitment and to display your gratitude to God?

YIELD

What does your prayer life produce in you? To what does it lead? What steps will you take now that you've studied Solomon's prayer?

In light of Scripture and based on your responses,
quiet yourself before the Lord and spend a few moments in prayer.

START

Welcome to group session 6 of *Praying at the Crossroads.*

Use the following questions to begin the session.

How would you describe your present spiritual life? Is it vital and full of life, or are you in a season of apathy, complacency, and dullness?

How would you describe the present spiritual climate in your church, community, state, and nation? Would you say we're in a season of spiritual famine, moral decline, and decay? If so, who's responsible for it?

What needs to happen for restoration to occur?

Never in recent history has there been a greater need for God's restoration through revival than today. The church desperately needs the Lord. Meanwhile, the church wastes away in sin, apathy, complacency, materialism, and arrogance. The church often wants to place the blame for this moral and spiritual collapse on political parties, economic downturns, racial tension, the lost world, and even the devil.

But in reality the body of Christ must own up to the fact that it's responsible. As James said, we've become friends of the world through our self-centeredness and self-reliance (prayerlessness; see Jas. 4:1-4). When this happens, spiritual apathy and complacency begin to increase. How can this downward spiral of spiritual famine be turned around?

We begin the journey toward restoration through desperation, humility, and brokenness before God. To humble ourselves before God requires great abandonment of self. It begins with us, not someone else. It begins in prayer with total surrender and dependence on the Lord who alone can restore our relationship with Him. That's why we desperately need to pray for God's restoration through revival before it's too late. This is what Joel 2 is all about: God's call to prayers that restore.[1]

Use these statements to follow along as you watch video session 6.

In Joel 1 the Lord was saying to His people, "Return to Me in godliness and holiness."

In Joel 2 God was continuing to pursue His people.

God's judgment and God's discipline were upon His people.

God called His people back to Himself because He wanted to restore His people.

God's invitation to His people was for them to return to Him, to desire Him, to love Him, and to seek Him through biblical repentance.

Application from Joel's Prayer

1. Turn away from rebellion and sin and turn to God.

2. Rend your heart.

3. Return to Him.

4. God wants to restore your relationship with Him.

Return describes running to the Lord.

You must want the Lord more than you want His blessings and deliverance.

God says, "You are a part of community. You are a part of the body. You are My people, and My people must return to Me."

God is calling His leaders to lead the people to pray toward His mercy.

This is a picture of God truly coming to be with His people.

We must come together and seek the Lord for His mercy because that's when God can truly restore us as His people.

Video sessions available at lifeway.com/prayingatthecrossroads or with a subscription to smallgroup.com

DISCUSS

Use the following questions to discuss the video teaching.

Read Joel 2 and discuss the following questions.

The prophet Joel, writing in the eighth or ninth century BC, relayed to a rebellious people God's deadline for His judgment on sin and His call for restoration. In Joel 1 Joel described the onslaught and devastation that a plague of locusts had brought on the inhabitants of Jerusalem. Despite the locusts, God's people continued in their sin. In Joel 2:1-11 Joel announced that an invading army from the north was approaching as God's discipline intensified. As before with the locusts, the devastation would be overwhelming and far-reaching.

"The LORD disciplines the one he loves" (Prov. 3:12). After reading Joel 2:1-11, how would you describe God's hand of discipline on His people?

How important is it for God's people to understand His perspective on sin? What are the implications if we don't acknowledge God's judgment and perspective?

God was drawing a line in the sand before His people. What should they do? How should they respond? Amid the physical and spiritual famine God invited His people to return to Him. Genuine biblical repentance was required (see vv. 12-13). Repentance included both brokenness over sin ("Tear your hearts," v. 13) and a wholehearted return to the Lord. Turning back to God was possible because the Lord is "gracious and compassionate" (v. 13). Contentment with His presence and restoration through relationship were the end goal, not His deliverance. His people must desire and trust Him above all (see v. 14).

What does the use of the phrase "Tear your hearts" in verse 13 say about the seriousness of God's call to repentance?

How do God's character traits mentioned in verse 13 encourage you to repent when you've sinned?

Verses 15-16 demonstrate that the call to repentance wasn't just personal but also corporate. This was a very urgent, serious invitation to gather and seek the Lord ("Announce a sacred fast," v. 15). Because God's people were up against His judgment, everyone was required to attend a sacred assembly. It was now or never. The congregation had to be sanctified (see v. 16) if the people were to experience the Lord's renewed presence, deliverance, and restoration.

> *Have you ever been a part of a sacred assembly in a local congregation? Discuss the significance of a sacred or solemn assembly in the life of a church.*

> *What do verses 15-16 teach us about the seriousness of corporate sin?*

This call to congregational purity was also a call for spiritual leaders to step up and lead God's people back to Him. Their role involved both personal and public brokenness over the nation's spiritual famine. The leaders were therefore to "weep between the portico and the altar" (v. 17), to humble themselves and lead God's people in desperate, united prayer for His mercy and intervention. God was their only hope as the surrounding nations mocked His people and asked, "Where is their God?" (v. 17).

> *How important is united prayer for God's mercy and intervention in your life and your church?*

> *What are you doing as a believer and/or as a leader to guide others toward desperate prayer for personal and corporate revival and spiritual awakening? What will you do?*

Joel 2:18-32 describes what can take place when God pours out His mercy on His people as they repent, return, and seek Him through humble, passionate, and desperate prayer. God heard their cries and returned to His people. As God's people pray and experience His restoration in the present, their hope and assurance in His future work of redemption and restoration are constantly being rekindled.

> *Give examples of ways God has restored you, your family, or your church as you've prayed during a seemingly hopeless situation.*

GROUP PRAYER

Use the following PRAY framework to pray together as a group.

In light of what we've studied today, pray together as a group, using the following prompts to guide your experience together. You'll repeat this exercise at the end of each day's personal study. Use the biblical prayer we studied to guide your own. Read each prompt aloud and encourage group members to lift up prayers based on these prompts silently or aloud, depending on their comfort level.

PRAISE *God for who He is and what He has done.*

God judged His people's sin through the locust plague and the approaching army from the north. He demonstrated His love for His people in the fact that He wouldn't allow them to continue in their rebellious ways. Praise God for disciplining and judging us as His people from a heart of love.

REPENT *of unconfessed sins and accept Christ's forgiveness.*

God invited His people to "tear" their hearts and "return" to the Lord (v. 13). Ask the Lord to identify any unconfessed sin or signs of a rebellious spirit in your heart and in your church. Then confess and repent before the Lord.

APPLY *the truths you've learned by committing to action.*

In Joel's day God wanted His people to seek Him, depend on Him, and want Him, not just His blessings, favor, and deliverance. Pray that the Lord will restore your desire to seek Him and His holy, manifest presence with and through you, not just His deliverance and blessings.

YIELD *your life to God's will and kind providence.*

In Joel's day God wanted to restore His people so that He could use them to make His name great among the nations. The same is true for His people today. Ask the Father to grant you the grace needed to seek Him and to lead others to seek His mercy and restoration through revival and spiritual awakening in your life, church, community, and nation.

Close by praying for specific requests that arose during the session.

GOD'S JUDGMENT AND PERSPECTIVE

Read Joel 2:1–11.

On the heels of the devastation wrought by the plague of locusts that's vividly described in Joel 1, chapter 2 begins with the sounding of the trumpet. In verse 1 it was used to sound the alarm that a "great and strong" northern army (v. 2) was approaching and would bring even more devastation and misery on God's people.

God's people had fear-filled hearts as they began to see the approaching army from the north. This verse paints the picture of people who suddenly realized they were about to face imminent danger and destruction, and they were horrified. The people's fear was coupled with the greater reality that God was against them (see v. 11). "If God is for us, who is against us?" (Rom. 8:31). But if God is against us, who can be for us? God wasn't with them. He was against them.

No one would endure this approaching army; no one can, and no one will . This warning is something to ponder today. What does it look like for God to be against us? We're beginning to see that more clearly as each day passes. We must ask the obvious questions: Are God's people even listening? God has been trying to get our attention for quite some time. Robert Coleman wrote these words in 1969—words that could have been written today:

> Men everywhere are sensing that something is missing in the life of the church. We have a form of religion but no power. ... Complacency is the norm. While the church flounders in mediocrity, the world plunges into sin. ... The sacredness of home and family is forsaken. ... But the day of reckoning is sure to come. Moral and spiritual decline has its limits. ... Already we are beginning to see the disintegration of enduring values in society, and unless something happens soon to change our course, civilization as we know it is on its way out.[2]

Despite the indicators and warnings, we continue in our sin, doing our own thing, maintaining our same misplaced priorities, and depending on self instead of God. Who will blow the trumpet? Who will listen? Prayers that restore are prayers that start with God and His perspective. Are you seeking that perspective?

PRAYER

Enter this time with your Bible and your heart open.
Based on the truths of Scripture, answer the following
questions and let them lead you to a time of prayer.

PRAISE

Have you ever experienced a time when you reached the end of your resources and were at a crossroads with God about your sin? Why should you praise God's intervening grace?

REPENT

Do you generally recognize God's hand of chastisement on your sin and disobedience? Reflect on your most recent time of confession and repentance with the Lord. Ask Him to show you your sin.

APPLY

Have you known people who didn't heed God's warnings? What was the outcome? What did God teach you from their mistakes?

YIELD

In what way is the Lord leading you to respond to the need for His people to wake up to the reality of His judgment and perspective?

In light of Scripture and based on your responses,
quiet yourself before the Lord and spend a few moments in prayer.

PERSONALLY REPENT AND RETURN

Read Joel 2:12-14.

Prayers that restore are prayers that flow from broken, repentant hearts. In verse 12 the word *now* shows the urgent need for the people to respond immediately to God's call for genuine repentance. The use of the phrase "this is the LORD's declaration" (v. 12) demonstrates God's loyal, patient love. Despite their rebellious state, God offered one more opportunity for His people to return to Him through repentance.

Turn (v. 12) points to the spiritual plight of the people of God; they were a distracted people. Perhaps they were looking at the devastation from the plague of locusts. Maybe their hearts were overwhelmed by the joyless people and mourning priests. Or perhaps they were so focused on self or their personal physical wants and needs that they had no interest in God's priorities.

The extent to which this turning must take place was "with all your heart" (v. 12). Whatever it took, they must turn and give their undivided attention to God. To ensure this wholehearted focus, they were also instructed to couple their turning to God "with fasting, weeping, and mourning" (v. 12).

In verse 13 *tear* described a rending action that usually referred to the ripping of cloth. This time it wasn't clothes that were to be torn but the people's hearts. This was a call to dig down to the root of the problem—their sin-stained, rebellious, distracted, and unforgiven hearts. No corner of the heart could be left untouched, and no sin could be ignored.

Once the heart was torn through contrition and brokenness, the time was ripe to return to the Lord and complete the act of repentance. The word *return* in verse 13 points to two ways: by turning away from their sin and returning to God.

"Who knows? He may turn and relent" (v. 14) poses a piercing question to God's people. On the surface we might think this verse paints a picture of people looking to heaven with a hopeful gaze that God would spare them from the approaching devastation. Yet God was seeking to drive home a deeper message: "It's really not about My coming to your aid and relenting of My anger toward you. I'm primarily concerned with My glory and your relationship with Me." When God's people get to the place where they're content with Him alone, they're at a place of complete trust.

PRAYER

Enter this time with your Bible and your heart open.
Based on the truths of Scripture, answer the following
questions and let them lead you to a time of prayer.

PRAISE

Have you recently given thanks to the Lord for His gracious, merciful love in Christ? How about His great kindness and patient spirit toward your sin?

REPENT

When was the most recent time you took more than a few seconds or minutes to allow God to search your heart for sin? We often confess our sin quickly and move on. Give God time to speak to you about your sin.

APPLY

Genuine biblical repentance starts with me: I need to repent! Take up the challenge to set aside a morning or an extended season before the Lord with nothing but His Word, a pen, and a sheet of paper. Ask Him to show you the true state of your heart before Him.

YIELD

When the Lord convicts you of sin, are you quick to repent? When you've sinned, do you long more for God's deliverance from the consequences of that sin or for God's renewed presence through a restored relationship?

In light of Scripture and based on your responses,
quiet yourself before the Lord and spend a few moments in prayer.

CORPORATELY REPENT AND RETURN

Read Joel 2:15-16.

There's always an outward or forward flow when God's people personally repent and return to Him. In verses 15-16 God called the entire congregation to return, refocus, rend their hearts, and repent. He wanted them to become His people—a mighty instrument of His presence and power through which He could flow.

In Joel's day the trumpet was used not only to warn the people of an approaching danger, as in verse 1, but also to summon God's people to a season of corporate fasting, worship, prayer, and consecration. The sacred or solemn assembly in verse 15 referred to an extended season of corporate worship and consecration that included the reading of God's Word, prayer, confession, repentance, and contrition before God.

The people were to gather and set themselves apart from sin and practices that weren't holy (see v. 16). This process occurred as they renewed their covenant relationship with God by setting up renewed boundaries based on God's standards of holiness as community. The force of the imperative command *sanctify* in verse 16 is strong, urgent, and intense, referring to a time when "all things are naked and exposed to the eyes of him to whom we must give an account" (Heb. 4:13). As a community of faith, God's people gathered to deal honestly and genuinely with the condition of their hearts before Him and one another. No one was exempt from this special season of seeking the Lord, not even children, nursing babies, and couples getting married (see v. 16). They were to pray for one another and hold one another accountable to the new boundaries that were set by God's standards.

There's no time to waste, nor is there time to blame others and ignore our sin. We must repent and return to the Lord for restoration. Prayers that restore will begin to be answered when God's people unite their hearts in genuine confession and repentance, with one accord seeking God and His renewed presence with them through a restored relationship. How will you and your congregation respond to this need?

PRAYER

Enter this time with your Bible and your heart open.
Based on the truths of Scripture, answer the following
questions and let them lead you to a time of prayer.

PRAISE

Is spiritual unity a recognizable attribute of your church? Is your church growing or declining?

REPENT

Does your church need revival and God's hand of restoration? Is your church suffering from the presence of unconfessed sin, a lack of holiness, or disobedience to God's commands?

APPLY

What kind of reputation does your church have in the community? What's keeping it from overcoming lostness in your community?

YIELD

Pray that a spirit of genuine repentance and humility before God will sweep through your church. Pray that your church will experience revival through God's hand of restoration.

In light of Scripture and based on your responses,
quiet yourself before the Lord and spend a few moments in prayer.

GOD'S MERCY AND RESTORATION

Read Joel 2:17.

Prayer that restores should be modeled by leaders who lead their families and churches to pray. In verse 17 God called the ministers, priests, and leaders to guide the people to desperately seek the Lord's mercy and restoration through passionate prayer.

Four aspects of this call to prayer stand out.
1. The leaders were to accept their responsibility to address the issue, pray, and lead the people in holiness and passionate prayer.
2. The leaders were to unite with other priests in this prayer effort.
3. The leaders were to model brokenness and desperation in prayer before the people.
4. The leaders were to cry out with specific, strategic prayers for God's mercy.

What can happen when spiritual leaders and pastors become broken over the spiritual famine in their hearts, their churches, and their land and lead the people to pray? Consider the historical example of Nicholas Ludwig von Zinzendorf. In late 1727 Zinzendorf became burdened because of the schisms that had formed among the religious refugees and believers from different traditions who sought asylum from persecution in Herrnhut.

This burden led Zinzendorf to pray and seek the Lord's guidance in leading the groups toward a united church community of love and oneness. Zinzendorf led the men to gather on August 13, 1727, to seek the Lord through confession, prayer, the study of Scripture, and holy communion. In that meeting God sent revival and stirred hearts toward continual spiritual renewal, oneness, and love, eventually giving birth to the Moravian Church movement. Zinzendorf started a continuous prayer emphasis that lasted more than one hundred years. The impact of prayer on the advancement of the Kingdom through the modern missionary movement will be known only in light of eternity.[3]

Today followers of Jesus must become broken over and take responsibility for the spiritual famine in the church and in the land. It's time to give great attention to a vibrant spiritual life and to prayer for God's restoration through revival. What will you and your church do?

PRAYER

Enter this time with your Bible and your heart open.
Based on the truths of Scripture, answer the following
questions and let them lead you to a time of prayer.

PRAISE

Why is it important for spiritual leaders to model a vital spiritual life and a life of prayer before other people? Identify spiritual leaders, past and present, who model a vital spiritual life before others.

REPENT

Joel 2:17 demonstrates that spiritual leaders must themselves be broken over the spiritual plight of individuals and congregations. Are you and leaders in your church broken over the spiritual famine in your life, church, community, and nation?

APPLY

Restoration can take place only because of God's great mercy. How will you actively engage in specific prayer efforts about the spiritual famine in your church and nation?

YIELD

Is the community around your church asking the question "Where is their God?" (v. 17)? Could God use you to gather other leaders and seek the Lord in passionate prayer for revival and spiritual awakening?

In light of Scripture and based on your responses,
quiet yourself before the Lord and spend a few moments in prayer.

HOPE AND TRUST IN RESTORATION

Read Joel 2:18-32.

When God's people repent and return to Him in holiness through relationship, they're in a position to experience His mercy and restoration through revival. In verses 18-19a the direction of the biblical text dramatically shifts in two important ways.

1. Joel used the word *then* (see v. 18) to begin his description of God's response to His people. The word refers to God's sovereign work of renewal and restoration that He was about to bring among His people. Because God is sovereign, He always determines when the *then* takes place, where it takes place, with whom it takes place, and to what extent it takes place. Thus, in this verse it signals that God was starting His work of restoration that would be accomplished in His way and in His time among His people.

2. The Lord began to speak directly to His people, rather than through Joel, about His plans to deliver and restore them. God had now relented from His wrath and had heard their prayers. He had come near to hear, speak, and be with them. God's manifest presence was now with them as He dwelled among His people.

In verses 18-32 the Lord described how far-reaching His restoration would be as He promised to spare his people (see v. 18), take away their reproach (see v. 19), remove the threat of devastation before His people (see v. 20), restore the years the locusts had eaten (see v. 25), and renew His presence with them (see v. 27). Furthermore, He promised a day when He would "pour out [His] Spirit on all humanity" (v. 28), providing salvation and deliverance for those who would call on His name (see vv. 28-32).

Prayers that restore are always grounded in our hope and trust in the Lord and in His sovereign grace and mercy, which are revealed in His redemptive work in Scripture and history through the living Christ. Hope for the future advancement of Christ's kingdom won't be found in any political, social, economic, or human solution but only in God's mercy and restoration through revival and spiritual awakening. When God revives His people, restoration will come, and America will begin to see the impact a revived church can have on lostness—but not until then. Come, Lord Jesus!

PRAYER

Enter this time with your Bible and your heart open.
Based on the truths of Scripture, answer the following
questions and let them lead you to a time of prayer.

PRAISE

Spend time reflecting on ways you've seen the Lord restore, save, and revive people and situations through answered prayer. Praise Him for His mercy and grace.

REPENT

Do you have difficulty believing God can truly restore and revive people and churches? Why or why not? Pray that you and your church will answer God's call to return to Him in godliness and holiness, crying out for His mercy and restoration in people's lives.

APPLY

Are you or is your church at a crossroads in your need for the Lord's restoration and renewal? If so, pray for growing hope and trust in the Lord to restore His church through revival.

YIELD

Could God use your church as a catalyst for revival and restoration in your region? What steps can you take to guide your church to become a catalyst for restoration and revival?

In light of Scripture and based on your responses,
quiet yourself before the Lord and spend a few moments in prayer.

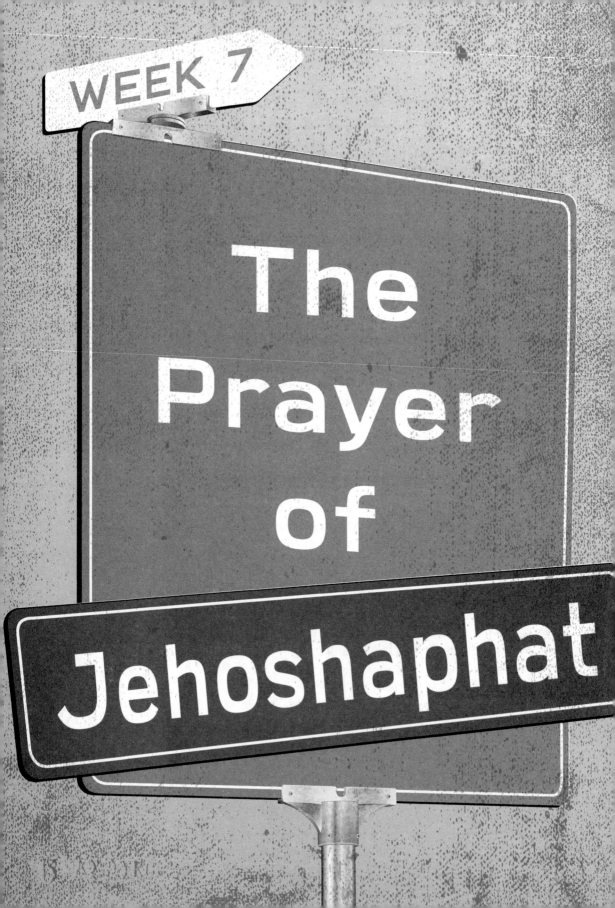

START

Welcome to group session 7 of *Praying at the Crossroads*.

Use the following questions to begin the session.

Identify a crisis that stirred deep fear in your heart.

How do you typically respond in a situation when you don't know what to do?

Does it seem to you that most people you know are either going through a crisis, have just come through a crisis, or face the prospect of an impending crisis? There's no question about it: life tests us, often with what appear to be insurmountable challenges. The way you respond to a crisis either uncovers the inadequacies of your personal resources or unveils the power of your faithful God. The difference depends on prayer.

If you face a significant threat in your life, an enemy lurking just over the hill, what Jehoshaphat did next should interest you. As we examine 2 Chronicles 20 this week, we'll see, understand, and put into practice the way he prioritized prayer, elevating it to a place of prominence as he responded to the danger before him. Jehoshaphat understood that nothing is impossible for the all-sufficient, all-powerful God of Abraham, Isaac, and Jacob. When faced with the impossible, he sought the Lord and found in Him the way to survive. Although initially fearful, Jehoshaphat turned his heart toward prayer and discovered power in praise.

Use these statements to follow along as you watch video session 7.

If we're a follower of Christ and we come to the place where we don't know what to do, the truth is, we *do* know what to do, and that is pray.

When we're afraid, we either run from God, trying to figure out our own solutions, or we run to God and find out what His solutions are.

Jehoshaphat gathered the whole people to communicate to them, "I'm your leader, but we are together in this."

Jehoshaphat, as the king, took the lead in praying for the people.

Jehoshaphat started this prayer with a sense of "Lord, You are the sovereign God. There is none like You."

We have to admit our helplessness.

Jehoshaphat fell on his face before the Lord God. All the court of the people bowed down on their faces before the Lord God, and recognizing that God was going to do a great thing among them, they cried out with praise to God.

God had answered the prayers, and He had led His people into times of praise.

When our fear becomes faith and our worry becomes worship, then our voices will be raised to God together in an adoration of the God who is the faithful, prayer-answering God.

Prayer and praise are always the appropriate response for anything that comes our way.

Video sessions available at lifeway.com/prayingatthecrossroads or with a subscription to smallgroup.com

DISCUSS

Use the following questions to discuss the video teaching.

Read 2 Chronicles 20:1-30.

What would you have expected Jehoshaphat to do when he heard the news of impending disaster?

During the reign of Judah's fourth king, Jehoshaphat, a massive enemy army approached Jerusalem from the southeast. After years of servitude to David, Solomon, and Asa, the people of Moab, Ammon, and Edom sensed that the time was right to fight for their independence from the kingdom of Judah. A messenger brought word of great danger to Jehoshaphat: "A vast number from beyond the Dead Sea and from Edom has come to fight against you" (2 Chron. 20:2). The threat was urgent; the joint forces of the enemy had already reached En-gedi, only twenty-five miles across the mountains. Faced with this threat, Jehoshaphat prayed.

How did Jehoshaphat's greatest fear force him to seek God with fervor? Do the fears and challenges you face turn you toward God or away from Him? Explain.

News of the threat posed by the approaching enemy armies hit Jehoshaphat particularly hard. He had faced this crisis before. When his father, Asa, was the king, a vast army from Ethiopia had attacked Judah. Before the day of battle arrived, Asa had cried out to the Lord in prayer:

> LORD, there is no one besides you to help the mighty and those
> without strength. Help us, LORD our God, for we depend on you,
> and in your name we have come against this large army. LORD,
> you are our God. Do not let a mere mortal hinder you.
> **2 CHRONICLES 14:11**

God answered Asa's prayer, and God's army routed the Ethiopians.

How did Asa's example shape Jehoshaphat's perspective on the priority of prayer as a first response to life's threats? Does your family learn more about worry or worship from the way you handle crises?

*Why do you think Jehoshaphat called on the entire nation to join him
in prayer (see 20:3-5)? How does his action reinforce Jesus' promise
in Matthew 18:19-20 for believers who agree in prayer?*

When we face overwhelming odds, a reliable biblical pattern of prayer begins
with rehearsing the Lord's character and perfections. In the first portion of
Jehoshaphat's prayer, he reminded himself and the gathered people that the
One to whom he was praying could handle even the most impossible situation
(see 2 Chron. 20:6-9).

*When you face the impossible, how do your prayers resemble or differ
from the way Jehoshaphat prayed?*

After he had expressed his confidence in God, Jehoshaphat then admitted
his own ignorance and impotence while confessing his total confidence that
God would show the nation what to do (see vv. 10-12).

*Why are we reluctant to let others know we don't know what to do?
How reluctant are you to confess your limitations to the Lord?*

In answer to Jehoshaphat's prayer, the Lord showed what He intended to
do through the prophet Jahaziel. After assuring the people that they didn't
need to be "afraid or discouraged" (v. 15), God revealed His plan. Judah
would march forth to meet their enemy, but they wouldn't have to lift their
hands in combat. Instead, they would lift their hands and voices in praise
and thanksgiving.

*When God's plan appears to be impractical and unsuited for the magnitude
of the challenge you face, what would make you trust Him rather than your
own solution?*

*Share a time when you experienced God's faithfulness in rescuing you from
insurmountable odds in a way that can be explained only by His direct
intervention.*

*What can you learn from Jehoshaphat's prayer about facing your fears
with faith and worship?*

GROUP PRAYER

Use the following PRAY framework to pray together as a group.

In light of what we've studied today, pray together as a group, using the following prompts to guide your experience together. You'll repeat this exercise at the end of each day's personal study. Use the biblical prayer we studied to guide your own. Read each prompt aloud and encourage group members to lift up prayers based on these prompts silently or aloud, depending on their comfort level.

PRAISE *God for who He is and what He has done.*
Review for a moment what it means that God is Lord of all creation, King of the nations of all the earth, and Sovereign over you and all crises you encounter. Praise Him that no challenge faces you that He can't overcome.

REPENT *of unconfessed sins and accept Christ's forgiveness.*
Confess times when you've tried to reason your way out of a difficult situation instead of praying for God's provision of guidance and deliverance. Then ask Him to forgive you for not trusting Him enough to set your heart on Him as your refuge and strength.

APPLY *the truths you've learned by committing to action.*
Call to mind anything you're currently worried or fearful about. Now, point by point, cast all of these burdens on God (see 1 Pet. 5:7).

YIELD *your life to God's will and kind providence.*
Tell the Lord you're wholeheartedly committed to do whatever He shows you without fear or reluctance. Then ask Him to open your eyes to see clearly through His Word what to do next, how to do it, and when to get started.

Close by praying for specific requests that arose during the session.

RESOLVED TO SEEK THE LORD

Read 2 Chronicles 20:1–13.

Because Jehoshaphat was the king, he was responsible for leading Judah to overcome its enemies in the name of the Lord. Even though he had seen what God did when his father, Asa, was the king, fear gripped him as he considered the magnitude of the threat facing him. Nothing in his experience prepared him to lead his people to withstand an invasion by such a large multitude. The way he managed his fear serves as a model for each of us when challenges threaten us.

In his fear Jehoshaphat "resolved to seek the LORD" (v. 3). Fear will turn us either to the Lord or away from the Lord. Jehoshaphat determined to do the former. Everyone who follows the Lord knows we should seek Him always. Why we don't do that mystifies us. We want to do it and intend to do it, yet our eyes drift elsewhere. For Jehoshaphat, shaken by the prospect of engaging in a battle he knew he couldn't win, fear cut through the fog and shaped his priorities.

Circumstances compelled Jehoshaphat to take action. Indecision wasn't an option in this case. The situation demanded action. Three immediate decisions distinguish Jehoshaphat as someone who closely walked with God.

1. Jehoshaphat proclaimed a fast in all the land of Judah (see v. 3). Fasting diverted the attention of the people away from their everyday distractions and focused it on the God who was their only hope.
2. Jehoshaphat gathered the people together (see v. 4). Throughout the land people traveled to Jerusalem not only to unite their voices in prayer but also to find strength in numbers and to seek the help only the Lord could give.
3. Jehoshaphat led the people in prayer (see vv. 4-12). He could have called on the religious leaders to preside, but in this time of crisis, it was better to lead by personal example in utter dependence on God. His words showed that he knew well the One to whom he spoke, the sovereign Lord of all.

Reflect for a moment on how magnificently God's sovereignty has been displayed in Jesus Christ. His resurrection was the master stroke by our sovereign God, for it proved Christ's glorious authority over life and death. It signaled His triumphant victory over sin on our behalf. Have you ever marveled at the grace you've received from the hand of the almighty Ruler of all?

PRAYER

Enter this time with your Bible and your heart open.
Based on the truths of Scripture, answer the following
questions and let them lead you to a time of prayer.

PRAISE

Reflect on God's power. Identify miraculous works recorded in Scripture revealing that nothing is impossible for Him. Praise Him for the way that truth can help you face your next challenge.

REPENT

When you question whether God can do what you think is impossible, you impugn His character. Ask Him to forgive your unbelief and to kindle faith in your heart to believe that He's always able.

APPLY

Determine that you'll act by faith in the power and sufficiency of Christ and take the first step in obeying His voice, whether through a specific word from Scripture or the leading of the Holy Spirit.

YIELD

Ask God to show you what He wants you to learn about His sovereign hand in your life. Ask Him to reveal the spiritual benefits your hard circumstances are bringing about in your life (see Rom. 8:28). Praise Him for His wisdom and ask Him to help you trust Him, for His thoughts and ways are different from yours (see Isa. 55:8-9).

In light of Scripture and based on your responses,
quiet yourself before the Lord and spend a few moments in prayer.

THE COVENANT-MAKING GOD

Read 2 Chronicles 20:7-12.

In leading the people of Judah in prayer, Jehoshaphat recounted the ways God had shown Himself to be a personal, loving God to His people. As you read the prayer again, notice three key themes on which he focused.

1. You're the God who keeps His covenants and has shown His power in the past (see v. 7). We aren't making an unfamiliar request in untested waters. You've already proved to be the covenant-keeping, all-powerful God.
2. You're the God whose presence is with us, whose temple stands among us (see vv. 8-9). Whenever we've faced trouble in the past, You were always near enough to hear our cries for deliverance. Your name is in this house, so we stand before You with humble confidence.
3. You're the God who now sees the enemy's threats (see vv. 10-12). Their offensive attacks stand as an egregious affront to Your mercy on them in the past. Surely Your judgment on them is justified, and Your favor to us is consistent with Your covenant faithfulness.

Anchoring his prayer in the character and might of the only true God, the covenant-making Sovereign God, Jehoshaphat appealed to what He personally knew, what Scripture affirmed, and what Judah's heritage of faith recorded. God is faithful. God is good. God is able.

The fear Jehoshaphat felt prompted him to gather the people and recount God's lovingkindness, goodness, and faithful works on their behalf. Because they knew who their God was, they bound themselves to Him in trust. Jehoshaphat humbly admitted his own helplessness and that of the people, basically confessing in verse 12, "God, I know these people expect me to get them out of this mess, but we all know the truth. We're clueless and powerless. Because You alone are all-knowing and all-powerful, our eyes are fixed on You."

As followers of Jesus Christ, we also enjoy the certainty of an everlasting covenant with God Himself. The covenant we have in Christ is actually an even better covenant than the one to which Jehoshaphat appealed. As the promised Messiah, Jesus Christ enacted a new, better covenant. Sin would be forgiven, and the indwelling, abiding presence of the Spirit would forever be assured (see Heb. 8:6-13). How much greater should our confidence be when we pray!

PRAYER

*Enter this time with your Bible and your heart open.
Based on the truths of Scripture, answer the following
questions and let them lead you to a time of prayer.*

PRAISE

Reflect on the difference Jesus has made in you since He came into your life.
Thank God for all of your spiritual blessings in Christ. Praise Him for His
grace and faithfulness in your life.

REPENT

Admit that you've failed to turn over certain portions of your life to Jesus'
lordship. Confess ways you've elevated worldly priorities over Him. Confess
ways you've turned back to worldly thoughts and actions. Ask Him to forgive
your unfaithfulness—for not loving Him with all your heart, soul, and mind.

APPLY

Meditate daily on the promises of God to you, His child in Jesus Christ. Look
at your difficult circumstances through the lens of these promises and keep
a record of the evidence of His grace and presence with you each day.

YIELD

Admit to the Lord, as Jehoshaphat did, that you're facing circumstances
you don't know how to handle. Then submit to Him by refusing to give in to
anxiety, instead praying with thanksgiving for His wisdom and faithfulness
until He gives you clarity about a particular direction He wants you to take
or a particular attitude He wants you to maintain.

*In light of Scripture and based on your responses,
quiet yourself before the Lord and spend a few moments in prayer.*

EXPECT AN ANSWER

> **Read 2 Chronicles 20:14-19.**

After praying and worshiping, the nation of Judah expected God to answer. When we've prayed and worshiped, we have to do what they did; we have to listen. God heard Jehoshaphat's prayer and responded. In their case God spoke through the prophet Jahaziel, giving him and the people hope and encouragement to face their fears with confidence. In our case He speaks through His Word by the Holy Spirit.

1. First they listened for instruction. Words of praise and thanksgiving went up to God. Then words to build their confidence came down from Him:

> Listen carefully, all Judah and you inhabitants of
> Jerusalem, and King Jehoshaphat. This is what the LORD
> says: "Do not be afraid or discouraged because of this
> vast number, for the battle is not yours, but God's.
> **2 CHRONICLES 20:15**

2. Next, knowing the Lord Almighty, their covenant-keeping God, was in their midst, the people took the only action that made sense. They fell down before Him and worshiped (see v. 18).

3. Finally, just as the people bowed down, the worship leaders, the Levites, stood up and began to praise the Lord with loud voices (see v. 19). Seldom will the Lord leave us on our faces. He humbles us by calling us to bend our knees before Him, but then His very presence with us causes us to rise up and praise Him with shouts of joy and words of exaltation. Psalm 22:3 declares that the Lord is "enthroned on the praises" of His people. We bow down in attitudes of wonder, then rise up in acts of worship.

With Judah's fears put into proper context before God, what earlier had them cowering in fear now appeared small when compared to the King of all creation, the Lord of heaven and earth. Jehoshaphat and the people could go to sleep that night with the peace of God guarding their hearts and minds (see Phil. 4:4-7). Worshiping instead of worrying always exalts His name and seals our peace.

PRAYER

Enter this time with your Bible and your heart open.
Based on the truths of Scripture, answer the following
questions and let them lead you to a time of prayer.

PRAISE

Name at least three ways God has shown Himself strong and sufficient on behalf of you or your family in the past. Praise and thank Him for His power and presence with you.

REPENT

When you question whether God cares about you because of your current circumstances, you're failing to trust in His proven character and promises. Ask Him to forgive you for listening to false thoughts about Him and failing to believe in His Word and His steadfast love for His children.

APPLY

As the choirs of Judah sang familiar psalms to express their gratitude and trust in God, choose a praise song or a psalm that expresses to Him your gratitude and trust. With "psalms, hymns, and spiritual songs" (Eph. 5:19), let your heart overflow with words and melodies of praise.

YIELD

Ask the Lord to open your eyes to see evidence of His lovingkindness and trustworthiness more clearly each day. Listen and let the Holy Spirit show you His faithfulness to you.

In light of Scripture and based on your responses,
quiet yourself before the Lord and spend a few moments in prayer.

FROM WORSHIP TO FAITH

Read 2 Chronicles 20:20–23.

Jehoshaphat encouraged the people to listen and believe all the prophet Jahaziel said. When the people went out to face the enemy the next morning, he urged them to trust (v. 20).

The God who had just spoken and was worthy of their worship was the God whose power to save could be trusted. Worship established the people's faith as they expressed what they believed and allowed those beliefs to shape their course of action toward the armies of the enemy.

The Lord had declared, "The battle is not yours, but God's" (v. 15). Jehoshaphat formulated the series of steps the people would take to gain a victory, steps only the Lord could orchestrate. From a human perspective, what he ordered his people to do bordered on insanity. But as an expression of faith by someone who knew how and what to pray, his battle plan allowed God's glory to shine brilliantly.

After consulting with the Lord in prayer and leading the people to do the same, Jehoshaphat explained the strategy they would employ against the enemy. Seldom do our prayers have such an immediate impact as Jehoshaphat's did. As you read verse 21, ask yourself how you would have reacted to Jehoshaphat's approach to the armed conflict they faced against a formidable force.

Think about it: "Put the singers before the soldiers and let's go to war!" That was the strategy born of Jehoshaphat's praying, worshiping, and listening to the Lord. Instead of armor the frontline troops would wear choir robes. Instead of weapons they would bear musical instruments. Instead of bloodthirsty battle cries to frighten the enemy, songs of thanksgiving and praise lauding God's everlasting lovingkindness would be on their lips. Their words offered thanks for the victory before they even engaged the enemy. Anyone can give thanks after the fact, but the design for this battle prescribed thanksgiving in advance. Because of the power of praise and their willingness to worship, Judah readied itself to follow its king as He followed the King of glory. All of that happened because people chose to pray instead of panic. Fear became faith when worry became worship.

PRAYER

Enter this time with your Bible and your heart open.
Based on the truths of Scripture, answer the following
questions and let them lead you to a time of prayer.

PRAISE

Express your gratitude to the Lord for speaking with precision and clarity
in His Word. Praise Him for every word He has preserved in Scripture to
grant us everything we need for "life and godliness" through His "very great
and precious promises" and eternal truths (2 Pet. 1:3-4).

REPENT

Tell God you're sorry for all of the times you've chosen not to believe
something He has specifically told you in His Word. Even though He said it,
you doubted it and sinned against Him. Now you can return to Him and ask
for His forgiveness and for greater faith to help your unbelief (see Mark 9:24).

APPLY

Meditate daily on the grace and lovingkindness of your Savior, Jesus Christ.
Determine to bring glory to His name by sharing the truth about God's love,
as seen in Jesus Christ, with a neighbor, coworker, or family member.

YIELD

Allow every fearful moment and every biblical mystery to serve as a call
to worship, reminding you that God's ways aren't your ways, His thoughts
are higher than your thoughts (see Isa. 55:8-9), and He's God and you're not.
These affirmations can begin to turn your worry into worship.

In light of Scripture and based on your responses,
quiet yourself before the Lord and spend a few moments in prayer.

PROVED TRUSTWORTHY

Read 2 Chronicles 20:24-30.

With the choir leading the way in song, the people went forward as the Lord had commanded. They didn't know what lay before them, but what they knew of God's power bolstered their confidence. Soon their faith became sight, and the Lord proved His trustworthiness right before their eyes.

As the people arrived at the vista overlooking the plain, they expected to encounter enemy armies. Instead, a panorama of carnage appeared (see v. 24). Indeed, God had prevailed without one weapon of Judah being lifted in conflict but with every voice in Judah being lifted in praise.

Consider what God had done for the people of Judah after they prayed and trusted Him with the outcome.

- God routed the enemy. As Judah marched through the mountain passes singing, the Lord moved through the enemy army with such power that not one man remained alive (see v. 24).
- God blessed Judah with extraordinary bounty. Instead of fighting, the people spent three days ferrying home the cargo left behind by the enemy, the spoils of victory (see v. 25).
- The blessing brought rejoicing. What had begun as one of the most fearful moments of their lives not only ended with relief but also turned into a time of exceeding joy: "All the men of Judah and Jerusalem turned back with Jehoshaphat their leader, returning joyfully to Jerusalem, for the LORD enabled them to rejoice over their enemies" (v. 27).
- News of God's greatness spread across the region. The dread of God fell on all of the surrounding nations when they heard what He had done to the enemies of Judah (see v. 29).
- Peace came to Jehoshaphat and Judah: "Jehoshaphat's kingdom was quiet, for his God gave him rest on every side" (v. 30).

Jehoshaphat proved to be a champion of prayer. He learned that God's revelation of His character prompts people of faith to run to Him when trouble comes.

PRAYER

Enter this time with your Bible and your heart open.
Based on the truths of Scripture, answer the following
questions and let them lead you to a time of prayer.

PRAISE

How has God delivered and helped you this week? How will you praise Him in light of His help?

REPENT

The Lord is our first line of defense. In what ways are you showing reluctance to trust Him and His goodness?

APPLY

The Lord makes it clear in His Word that He's looking for men and women of faith He can count on to seek Him above all else. Will He find that kind of faith in you?

YIELD

Because the people trusted God and obeyed His words, they could stand and see salvation. How will you stand in the confidence of God's blessing today?

In light of Scripture and based on your responses,
quiet yourself before the Lord and spend a few moments in prayer.

WEEK 8

The Prayer of Hezekiah

START

Welcome to group session 8 of *Praying at the Crossroads*.

Use the following questions to begin the session.

Have you ever had to deal with a bully? Have you ever been terrorized by someone or something that seemed determined to harm you?

How did you respond? What ideas came to mind as you sought to rid yourself of the trouble? To whom or what did you turn for help?

Threats are a part of this fallen world, and they stalk us in many forms. Sometimes the threat is a person who's intent on harming us. Other threats are impersonal, such as illness or natural disasters, which indiscriminately wreak havoc in people's lives. No matter who you are, where you live, what your economic status is, or what your religious life is like, troublemakers will find you. A Christian's response in the face of such realities may tend toward panicking or devising a plot to make things better. Sadly, the last course many of us choose is prayer.

Rather than panicking, plotting, or using persuasion, the Bible urges prayer in times of trouble. In fact, prayer should be our first response and not our last resort. A wonderful portion of Scripture that drives this point home is 2 Kings 18–19, which concerns a man named Hezekiah. His story reveals that prayer does what no plotting or persuasiveness can do.

Use these statements to follow along as you watch video session 8.

The Scriptures would urge us to make prayer a first instinct rather than a last resort.

The beginning of prayer is humility, dependence on God.

God, my problem is now Your problem.

Start with God's glory, not with your gimme.

Prayer is asking God for something.

In prayer we realize that we are not alone. Our problems are not ours alone, but God comes in and takes them from us.

Application from Hezekiah's Prayer

1. Pray.

2. BOW:

- Bless God first.

- Open. Pray with an open Bible.

- Wants. Tell God what you want.

Want what you want, but want what God wants more than what you want.

*Video sessions available at lifeway.com/prayingatthecrossroads
or with a subscription to smallgroup.com*

DISCUSS

Use the following questions to discuss the video teaching.

In 2 Kings 18–19 we learn about a man named Hezekiah, who at twenty-five years of age became the king of Judah.[1] He was one of Israel's better kings. Chapter 18 provides his résumé.

- He did what was right in the Lord's sight (see v. 3).
- He uprooted kingdomwide idolatry (see v. 4).
- He trusted in the Lord and held fast to him (see vv. 5-6).
- He was accomplished on the battlefield (see vv. 7-8).

Even a man this highly regarded in Scripture faced a menacing terror, namely the Assyrian Empire.

What can we learn from Hezekiah about the nature of trouble even in the life of the godly?

Are you inclined to believe your faithfulness to God should exempt you from attacks and trials?

The remainder of chapter 18 (see vv. 9-37) introduces us to the Assyrians, who were the biggest bullies on the block during Hezekiah's day. They were known for a policy of frightfulness. Assyria brutalized, terrorized, and tormented other nations. Often they impaled victims as a means of psychological warfare. The biblical account is supported by historical documents that depict the Assyrians as "an aggressive, murderously vindictive regime supported by a magnificent and successful war machine."[2] So understandably, Hezekiah was shaken when this empire set its sights on Judah.

As God's people, we face antagonism from various sources. We must remember that ultimately, "our struggle is not against flesh and blood, but against the rulers, against the authorities, against the cosmic powers of this darkness, against evil, spiritual forces in the heavens" (Eph. 6:12). Why is it important to remain aware of this foe and his schemes?

Under King Shalmaneser, Hezekiah watched Assyria defeat and deport his brothers, the Northern Kingdom of Israel (see 2 Kings 18:9-12). Now under a new bully, Sennacherib, Hezekiah and the Southern Kingdom were under attack (see v. 13).

What was Hezekiah's initial response to the Assyrian threat (see vv. 14-16)? What was wrongheaded about his response?

When faced with opposition, why do we often turn to human means before we place our trust in God?

What are your tendencies when you face attacks?

Hezekiah didn't pray immediately, but after an unsuccessful attempt at "Let's make a deal," he pivoted from bargaining to bowing. In chapter 19 Hezekiah stopped trying to pay his way out and decided to pray his way out. His prayer is recorded in 2 Kings 19:15-19, and verses 35-37 demonstrate that his prayer was successful. What his plotting and persuading didn't accomplish, his prayer did. Assyria retreated, and Sennacherib was killed through a divine booby trap in response to Hezekiah's prayer.

When the Reformer Martin Luther wrote "A Mighty Fortress Is Our God," he wrote of the "ancient foe" being defeated by "one little word." One word of prayer is certainly effective enough to "fell him."[3] The Lord fights our battles for us and welcomes us to call on Him in times of trouble. We aren't sufficient on our own, but the Lord Jesus has already won the battle. Hezekiah teaches us that prayer does what neither our panicking, plotting, nor persuasiveness can do.

Think about the struggles you're facing. Which ones could benefit from more prayer? Who will join you in praying?

GROUP PRAYER

Use the following PRAY framework to pray together as a group.

In light of what we've studied today, pray together as a group, using the following prompts to guide your experience together. You'll repeat this exercise at the end of each day's personal study. Use the biblical prayer we studied to guide your own. Read each prompt aloud and encourage group members to lift up prayers based on these prompts silently or aloud, depending on their comfort level.

PRAISE *God for who He is and what He has done.*
Praise God for the privilege and power of prayer. Thankfully praise Him for His invitation "Let us approach the throne of grace with boldness, so that we may receive mercy and find grace to help us in time of need" (Heb. 4:16).

REPENT *of unconfessed sins and accept Christ's forgiveness.*
Repent for moments and seasons of prayerlessness. One preacher has rightly noted, "The greatest tragedy of life is not unanswered prayer, but unoffered prayer."[4] Begin taking everything to your Father in prayer. Take your fears, challenges, and enemies to Him in prayer, seeking His strength and solutions.

APPLY *the truths you've learned by committing to action.*
Apply the truth of this biblical account to your earthly and spiritual life. We may need the Lord to defeat not only earthly enemies but also the bully of sin in our lives. Record the top five troublemakers in your life and lay them before the Lord in prayer. Then stand and be amazed by what the Lord will do.

YIELD *your life to God's will and kind providence.*
Yield to God's timetable. The Lord is faithful but often not as punctual as we would like. As you trust Him for His plans for your life, also trust His timing. He will get the victory in such a way that He gets the glory.

Close by praying for specific requests that arose during the session.

A GODWARD ORIENTATION

Read 2 Kings 18:1-8.

The Bible says, "The prayer of a righteous person is very powerful in its effect" (Jas. 5:16). In other words, effective prayers are by-products of a godly life. When 2 Kings 18 introduces us to King Hezekiah, it describes him as a man deeply committed to Yahweh. Verses 3-8 detail some of his key efforts to restore kingdomwide faithfulness to Yahweh. So when we encounter Hezekiah's prayer in chapter 19, we know it wasn't made by someone who prayed only when times were hard. Hezekiah prayed from an authentic, consistent relationship with God.

Hezekiah's fidelity to Yahweh is presented in stark contrast to many of the kings in Israel's history. His own father, Ahaz, "did not do what was right in the eyes of the LORD ... but walked in the ways of the kings of Israel" (16:2-3). In 2 Kings 17:7-20 we learn that Israel's continual unfaithfulness to Yahweh resulted in judgment. In contrast, Hezekiah is described as being like David in his loyalty to God and His agenda (see 18:3).

King Hezekiah began his reign by launching an all-out assault on idolatry and false worship. He "removed the high places, shattered the sacred pillars, and cut down the Asherah poles. He broke into pieces the bronze snake that Moses made, for until then the Israelites were burning incense to it" (v. 4). According to a parallel account, Hezekiah also repaired the temple, offered extensive dedicatory sacrifices when the renovation was complete, and celebrated Passover (see 2 Chron. 29–31).

The key to Hezekiah's piety and productivity was twofold.
1. On one hand, Hezekiah "relied on the LORD" and "remained faithful to the LORD and did not turn from following him but kept the commands the LORD had commanded Moses" (2 Kings 18:5-6).
2. Even more fundamentally, "The LORD was with him" (v. 7). Hezekiah's heart was bent toward God as a reflection and a result of God's commitment to him.

Hezekiah's relationship with Yahweh produced a spiritual root from which the spiritual fruit of courage emerged. Courageously, he "rebelled against the king of Assyria and did not serve him" (v. 7). Hezekiah also demonstrated the instinct to pray. Hezekiah's story reminds us that prayer is not only important but also the instinct of people who truly know God.

PRAYER

Enter this time with your Bible and your heart open.
Based on the truths of Scripture, answer the following
questions and let them lead you to a time of prayer.

PRAISE

Praise God for cultivating godly character in you. The Bible exhorts you
to "work out your own salvation with fear and trembling. For it is God who
is working in you both to will and to work according to his good purpose"
(Phil. 2:12-13). Pray for a continued inner thirst and resolve to champion His
agenda and to contend against forces and causes that oppose his kingdom
purposes.

REPENT

A hallmark of Hezekiah's reign was his assault on idolatry. What idols, sinful
practices, or tendencies that oppose Christ do you need to repent of in your
heart, home, and/or church?

APPLY

Hezekiah's Godward orientation affected not only him personally but also the
people under his leadership. What specific principles and/or practices can be
instituted in your life that would help cultivate a climate of overall spiritual
faithfulness and provide a compelling Christian witness?

YIELD

This passage of Scripture reveals that spiritual commitment and convictions
in the Christian life are crucial. John 15 describes this dynamic as abiding in
Christ. Often we neglect to understand prayer as a part of a broader spiritual
life. Prayer can be a shot in the dark rather than springing from a consistent
walk in the light. With God's help will you commit to a disciplined, active
prayer life?

In light of Scripture and based on your responses,
quiet yourself before the Lord and spend a few moments in prayer.

PRAYER: THE BELIEVER'S OFFENSE

Read 2 Kings 18:9-18.

After verses 1-8 provide a favorable view of King Hezekiah's life and reign, the text shifts to his face-off with the ruthless empire of Assyria. Hezekiah had witnessed the Assyrian king Shalmaneser conquer and deport his brothers, the Northern Kingdom of Israel (see vv. 10-11). Now in the fourteenth year of his reign, he and Judah were being attacked by the new Assyrian king, Sennacherib. In fact, Sennacherib "attacked all the fortified cities of Judah and captured them" (v. 13). This threat was undeniable, and it was no joke.

Hezekiah's first strategy was to try finding a solution to make the problem go away. He sought to bargain and even submit to the more powerful foe (see vv. 14-16). He sought to pay off Sennacherib, even taking resources devoted to the mission and glory of Yahweh and offering them to the godless king as appeasement. This is often our initial instinct: to look within or to look around for the help that can come only from above.

Needless to say, God wouldn't allow Hezekiah's efforts to bring about the desired result of deliverance. Assyria didn't relent but rather took the payoff while increasing the pressure and furthering the attack (see vv. 17-18). The representatives of Sennacherib proclaimed him to be "the great king, the king of Assyria" (v. 19), and Hezekiah treated him as such. By seeking to appease Sennacherib rather than appeal to the true God and King, Hezekiah gave glory to the wrong king.

Instead of wishing, worrying, or trying to work something out, we're invited to pray. In the New Testament Paul said:

> Don't worry about anything, but in everything, through prayer
> and petition with thanksgiving, present your requests to God.
> **PHILIPPIANS 4:6**

Paul rightly saw prayer as a weapon, our first line of offense. You've heard the saying "The best defense is a good offense." Prayer is a great offense, so let's pray.

PRAYER

Enter this time with your Bible and your heart open.
Based on the truths of Scripture, answer the following
questions and let them lead you to a time of prayer.

PRAISE

God is shown to be exalted in our lives when we turn to Him and no other
"saviors"—family, friends, business partners, experts, and specialists. Whom
or what are you prone to seek out when you're in trouble or need? If you
could avert trouble without prayer, would you?

REPENT

A T-shirt reads, "When all else fails, pray." Prayer shouldn't be a last resort
but an initial reflex. Repent for praying only after all else fails.

APPLY

Prayer is the primary application of these verses. Sometimes we talk about
prayer without actually praying. What issues do you need to take to the
Father?

YIELD

These verses remind us that God has issued a standing invitation to take
every matter, big and small, to Him in prayer. One kind of prayer is petition,
which is making your specific requests known to God. Enter a time of specific
petition, expressing your total trust in His ability and kindness.

In light of Scripture and based on your responses,
quiet yourself before the Lord and spend a few moments in prayer.

DAY 3

WHOM OR WHAT DO YOU TRUST?

Read 2 Kings 18:19–37.

Prayer, at its core, is a matter of trust. When we pray, we turn away from depending on ourselves to the only One who can be trusted to answer our prayers. In verses 19-20 the Assyrian royal spokesman asked Hezekiah some profound questions:

> What are you relying on? You think mere words
> are strategy and strength for war. Who are you now
> relying on so that you have rebelled against me?
> **2 KINGS 18:19–20**

Hezekiah had tried to cooperate with the intimidator Sennacherib to no avail. Sennacherib didn't want a truce; he wanted to trounce Hezekiah and the people of Judah. Hezekiah would have to pivot from his previous efforts to prayerfully trusting God.

The questions must have reverberated in Hezekiah's mind. Whom would he trust? This question must be answered by God's people of all ages: "Who are you now relying on?" (v. 20). Don't miss the all-important word *now*. Past belief and future belief would be of little avail if belief weren't present right now.

On the surface it seems apparent that Hezekiah had no human help at his disposal. Therefore, the arrogant Assyrian king repeatedly taunted him, terrorized the people of Judah, and even blasphemed Yahweh. Sennacherib scoffed at the notion that Hezekiah had either military or spiritual resources to stand against his threat. He even offered himself as their only hope (vv. 31-32).

Sennacherib was partly right in assessing the weakness of Hezekiah and the people of Judah, but he greatly erred in assuming their God couldn't and wouldn't deliver them. Assyria had come against underdogs before but never against one that had Yahweh as its defender. Sennacherib would meet more than his match. He would meet his Maker.

This is a good word for God's people when we face terrors and terrorists of any magnitude. Instead of looking within or looking around, in faith we can confidently pray.

PRAYER

Enter this time with your Bible and your heart open.
Based on the truths of Scripture, answer the following
questions and let them lead you to a time of prayer.

PRAISE

Praise the Lord who can never fail and will never disappoint. Your health, wealth, friends, and family will almost certainly fall short at some point in your life. Praise God for His dependability and for being willing and able "to do above and beyond all that we ask or think" (Eph 3:20).

REPENT

Repent for dishonoring the Lord Jesus by trusting in other people and things. Can you think of times and particular circumstances when you displayed greater reliance on yourself and others than on Christ, the solid rock?

APPLY

Sometimes we may more readily trust God for eternal matters but not earthly matters. Trust Him not only for eternal life but also for every need each day. Meditate on Romans 8:32:

> He did not even spare his own Son but offered him up for
> us all. How will he not also with him grant us everything?"
> **ROMANS 8:32**

YIELD

The world will solicit your trust, and you may be especially tempted to trust in yourself. What are you currently depending on to improve your position in life? Submit to God's admonition in Proverbs 3:5:

> Trust in the LORD with all your heart,
> and do not rely on your own understanding.
> **PROVERBS 3:5**

In light of Scripture and based on your responses,
quiet yourself before the Lord and spend a few moments in prayer.

HUMILITY: THE KEY TO PRAYER

Read 2 Kings 19:1–13.

How do you pray? Prayer has a distinct posture. Some merely throw up a wing and a prayer with little or no true faith (see Jas. 1:5-8). Others pray with a sense of self-righteousness or entitlement, like the Pharisee in Luke 18:10-14. The right way to pray is with a humble posture. In prayer we should get low as we look up.

Second Kings 19 opens with King Hezekiah in a very humble position. This is the best position for prayer. When Hezekiah seemed to be at his weakest, he displayed a crucial strength: humility before the Lord.

Honestly, Hezekiah's lowly posture might have been motivated, in large part, by the troubling circumstances. Recall that he had initially tried to cooperate and even bargain with Sennacherib (see 18:13-16). Now the text says, "When King Hezekiah heard their report [the Assyrians' taunts and threats], he tore his clothes" (19.1). Our troubles are sometimes God's merciful way of producing the prayerful posture we need.

If you can even remotely relate to Hezekiah at this point, let the Bible encourage you. On the surface it seemed that in comparison to Sennacherib, Hezekiah couldn't have been a weaker opponent. However, Hezekiah had become so totally convinced of his inadequacy that he turned to his all-sufficient Savior.

Assyria would continue its bullying tactics, but Hezekiah was comforted and strengthened by the word that came back from the prophet Isaiah (see vv. 6-7). Isaiah assured Hezekiah that the danger he faced would dissipate. Hezekiah's humility stood in stark contrast to Assyria's arrogance. In prayer there's no place for pride, only for getting low and looking up.

Threats, however, don't simply vanish because we're humble. Hezekiah continued to be bombarded with Sennacherib's threats. An unrelenting barrage of hostile rhetoric was aimed at Judah, Hezekiah, and his God.

The Lord draws near to the lowly. This truth is the key to prayer. Those who trust in Christ's power can say, "When I am weak, then I am strong" (2 Cor. 12:10). Hezekiah's weakness made him eligible for divine strengthening. We'll see in the next lesson how his humble posture was combined with his dependent prayer.

PRAYER

Enter this time with your Bible and your heart open.
Based on the truths of Scripture, answer the following
questions and let them lead you to a time of prayer.

PRAISE

If you don't pray as much or as often as you would like, divine providence can use circumstances to ensure that you do. Praise the Lord for being loving enough to humble you when necessary and faithful enough to draw near to you when you're weak and lowly. Instead of complaining, praise God for causing you to go low and depend on Him so that you can receive His divine help.

REPENT

Are you trusting in your own strength? Are you trusting in another person's strength? Repent for times when you failed to humbly position yourself before God. Repent for times when you prayed with a sense of entitlement rather than with a spirit of dependence.

APPLY

When was the most recent time you bowed in prayer? Stretch out before the Lord and lay your concerns before Him in total surrender.

YIELD

Yield to God's work in your life to bring you low enough for Him to provide His strength.

In light of Scripture and based on your responses,
quiet yourself before the Lord and spend a few moments in prayer.

THE GOD WHO CARES

Read 2 Kings 19:14–37.

Prayer works. This fact is a major incentive to pray. Even though our prayers don't need to be fancy to be effective, we, like Jesus' disciples, must be taught to pray (see Matt. 6:5-15; Luke 11:1-13). Hezekiah's prayer, recorded in 2 Kings 19:14-19, provides a helpful model of biblical prayer. Furthermore, verses 35-37 document its effectiveness. Lord willing, this biblical account of Hezekiah will inspire you to confidently devote yourself to prayer.

Hezekiah began his prayer by taking the letter with Sennacherib's words and spreading it before the Lord (see v. 14). It was as though he were saying in faith, "God, take it; this is Your problem now." And that's just what Hezekiah did.

Next Hezekiah ascribed to Yahweh the glory and honor due to Him, while acknowledging His universal rule over heaven and earth (see v. 15). Prioritizing God's glory and agenda is the only right way to proceed in prayer. We shouldn't aim to bend God to our will but to align our will with His. Notice too that Hezekiah's prayer was preeminently rooted in the glory of God (see vv. 15-16). Only secondarily did Hezekiah turn the focus to the nation's well-being (see vv. 17-19).

Hezekiah's petition is deeply theological yet strikingly simple. Remember, God isn't looking for eloquence in our prayers but humble dependence. Hezekiah simply prayed, "Listen closely, LORD, and hear" (v. 16). Prayer seeks an audience with the God who's paying attention. The good news is that He knows what we need before we ask (see Matt. 7:7; John 16:24).

Next Hezekiah cried out, "LORD our God, please save us" (2 Kings 19:19). This is a short, succinct request, and Hezekiah's motive is made clear: "so that all the kingdoms of the earth may know that you, LORD, are God—you alone" (v. 19). In verses 20-34 Isaiah predicted Assyria's downfall, and the fulfillment of his prophecy is recorded in verses 35-37. Hezekiah received an answer to his prayer, the deliverance he humbly sought on his knees.

The God to whom we pray is supremely exalted, all-powerful, attentive, concerned, loving, and just. Jesus conquered the biggest bully of all—death—so you can trust Him for anything and everything. Cast your cares on Jesus because He cares for you (see 1 Pet. 5:7).

PRAYER

Enter this time with your Bible and your heart open.
Based on the truths of Scripture, answer the following
questions and let them lead you to a time of prayer.

PRAISE

The God who's enthroned in heaven cares about what His people are experiencing on earth. Praise the Father, who invites you to cast your cares on Him because He cares.

REPENT

Can you recall times when you displayed greater reliance on yourself and concern for your affairs than for the glory of God? Repent for first seeking your kingdom rather than the kingdom of God and His righteousness.

APPLY

Apply the acronym BOW.

- *Bless.* Bless God. Begin your prayer by acknowledging the supremacy of God and His glory. Jesus told us to pray, "Your name be honored as holy" (Matt. 6:9).
- *Open.* Pray with an open Bible or as though it were. You can literally pray with an open Bible or simply pray God's Word back to Him. Pray in light of what He has revealed in Scripture.
- *Wants.* Tell the Father what you want. Be willing to accept what He wants if it's not what you want. Remember Jesus' prayer before going to the cross: "Not my will, but yours, be done" (Luke 22:42). Let the words often voiced by the great missionary Jim Elliot comfort you: "God always gives His best to those who leave the choice with Him."[5]

YIELD

Yield to God's Word, which bids you to deny yourself (see Matt. 16:24), while at the same time urging you to make your requests known to God with thanksgiving (see Phil. 4:6).

In light of Scripture and based on your responses,
quiet yourself before the Lord and spend a few moments in prayer.

START

Welcome to group session 9 of *Praying at the Crossroads*.

Use the following questions to begin the session.

Recall a time in your life when you questioned why God was allowing your circumstances to occur. How did you respond? What did you do to resolve your questions?

When facing questions you couldn't answer, have you ever responded to God in an unproductive way? What should you have done differently?

Are you carrying a burden, or have you done so in the past? The first word of the Book of Habakkuk can be translated as either "oracle" or "burden." The contents of the book demonstrate that Habakkuk was definitely carrying a burden. Verse 2 says in response to his burden, Habakkuk prayed. That's the best response to a burden. But in his prayer Habakkuk accused God of being inattentive ("You do not listen") and indifferent ("You do not save").

What did Habakkuk see that caused him to question God? Verses 3 refers to "injustice," "wrongdoing," "oppression and violence," "strife," and "conflict." If we're paying attention to what's going on around us, we can identify with Habakkuk. We see lawlessness, a lack of respect for the rule of law, and surely as much wrongdoing as Habakkuk saw. When we see these crimes, with Habakkuk we sometimes ask God:

> Why do you force me to look at injustice?
> Why do you tolerate wrongdoing?
> **HABAKKUK 1:3**

In other words, "Why is the world like this? Why do I have to look at this sin every day?" The way Habakkuk dealt with his questions and moved toward resolving them provides direction for us when we ask similar questions.

Use these statements to follow along as you watch video session 9.

If we pray only when we understand things, only when times are good for us, there are going to be some significant gaps in our prayer lives.

God already knows what we're thinking and what we're feeling, so why not talk to Him about it?

Habakkuk was asking, "How can a good God allow evil, injustice, and suffering in the world?"

Application from Habakkuk's Prayer

When we don't understand our circumstances …

1. We return to God's presence.
2. We review what we know about God's character.
3. We remember that the righteous will live by faith.
4. We respond by praising God.

The time when we're walking through difficulty is the time when we need God more than at any other time.

Attributes of God That Habakkuk Affirmed

- Eternality
- Holiness
- Sovereignty over history
- Purity

Habakkuk was sure about some bedrock truths about God, and he stood on that.

Even though everything goes wrong in my life, I will still rejoice in God, the One who has saved me.

The more we know God, the more we will want to praise Him.

DISCUSS

Use the following questions to discuss the video teaching.

Read the Book of Habakkuk.

Why did Habakkuk go to God in prayer when he didn't understand his circumstances? What are some benefits of praying at such times?

What's the difference between going to God in prayer to express our frustration or complaint and questioning God's goodness and sovereignty? How is one spiritually healthy and the other unhealthy?

Typically, what ways of God are we able to understand, and what ways are beyond our understanding?

Why should we express praise in a time of questioning? What's the value of such praise?

When we love people, we want to spend time with them. When we're struggling, we want to talk with the one we love and trust most. If we love and trust God most, prayer will be our natural response when we're struggling to understand difficult circumstances. During such circumstances many people talk about God, but they don't talk with Him. Talking with God at such times involves honestly telling Him our feelings, listening to Him speak to us from Scripture, and obediently responding to His Word. Through such a process we may not receive definitive explanations of our circumstances, but we'll know God and His ways better.

Observing Habakkuk's honest struggle and response should help us see that we can approach God and communicate with Him during difficult circumstances. Though at times we're tempted to run away from God during these times, Habakkuk shows us that God can always be trusted.

Why are prayer and praise essential disciplines when we struggle with questions and doubts?

The Book of Habakkuk demonstrates that God wants us to come to Him in prayer even when we have questions and frustrations. Though Habakkuk questioned, he kept talking with God. As a result, he gained spiritual strength and grew in his knowledge of and trust in God.

> *What's your daily and weekly routine of prayer? When you've faced difficulties that confused you, did your questions change the frequency of prayer? Did your questions change the content of your prayers?*

In the Bible, people like Jeremiah and Job questioned God's justice in allowing them to suffer. Habakkuk questioned God's justice in judging sinful Judah by pointing out the greater sins of Babylon. But even in their questioning, each man continued to talk with God. They didn't complain *about* God; they complained *to* God.

> *Habakkuk told God, "You do not listen" (1:2). Have you ever felt God wasn't listening to you? What assurances do we have that God hears us when we pray?*
>
> *Saying, "You do not save" (v. 2) to God approaches blasphemy. What causes people to speak such words to God? Why are we certain God saves? Under what conditions does He save?*
>
> *Have you ever shared an experience of doubt or questioning with someone who isn't yet a Christian? How can such an experience be used as a witness of God's grace in the gospel?*

In our walk with God we can be honest with Him. When we question His ways, He knows, so why not talk with Him about what's in our hearts? Going to God with our thoughts, even when we're doubting, reminds us that we're children of God and dependent on Him.

GROUP PRAYER

Use the following PRAY framework to pray together as a group.

In light of what we've studied today, pray together as a group, using the following prompts to guide your experience together. You'll repeat this exercise at the end of each day's personal study. Use the biblical prayer we studied to guide your own. Read each prompt aloud and encourage group members to lift up prayers based on these prompts silently or aloud, depending on their comfort level.

PRAISE *God for who He is and what He has done.*

We don't always understand what God is doing in our lives, but God's character doesn't change, and His plan is always good. Praise God that His ways aren't our ways (see Isa. 55:8-9). He's greater than we are in every way. Praise God that His good purpose will triumph in the end.

REPENT *of unconfessed sins and accept Christ's forgiveness.*

A lack of understanding isn't sin, nor is asking a question. We sin when we fail to acknowledge that God is in control, that His plan is good, and that His ways are holy. Confess any neglect to submit to God as the sovereign Lord of your circumstances.

APPLY *the truths you've learned by committing to action.*

Habakkuk confessed to God exactly what he was thinking. Be honest about your current thoughts about God and His ways. Commit to talk with God about all of your thoughts.

YIELD *your life to God's will and kind providence.*

Even when we can't see or understand what God is doing, He's at work, and His work is always good. God will cause justice and righteousness to win in the end. Tell God that you're submitting to Him and trusting Him to care for you eternally even when you don't understand your current circumstances.

Close by praying for specific requests that arose during the session.

SUBMITTING TO GOD AND HIS WAYS

Read Habakkuk 1:1–11.

News stories confront us almost constantly. We see them on Twitter, in our email inbox, on Internet news feeds, and on the TV news. And we don't see much good news. We see reports of violent crimes, strife between people, and corruption of all kinds. Maybe you feel like praying with Habakkuk, asking God why so much injustice exists (see v. 3) Habakkuk saw sin all around him, he didn't want to see it, and he wondered why God wasn't doing something about it.

Habakkuk wasn't alone in asking God how long He would allow injustice (see v. 2). Believers in the one true God have always struggled with the presence of injustice in a world created and governed by our just God.

Verses 5-11 record God's answer to Habakkuk. God told Habakkuk that He was going to judge sinful Judah with an attack by the Chaldeans, or Babylonians. That answer hardly eliminated Habakkuk's question.

Why does God use unrighteous people, like the Babylonians, to do His work? If we rephrase that question, we may be shocked by our own impertinence: "God, why are You gracious to sinners? Why are You patient with the ungodly?" Instead of questioning the way God administers justice, perhaps we should give God praise that He's gracious and patient with us.

Second Peter 3:9 says:

> The Lord does not delay his promise, as some
> understand delay, but is patient with you, not
> wanting any to perish but all to come to repentance.
> **2 PETER 3:9**

God doesn't eliminate all sin, because He's not ready to eliminate all sinners. He's patient and wants them to repent.

Thanking God for the patience and grace He has shown to us in the gospel strengthens our prayer lives. Our relationships with God are also deepened when we confess to Him that we can't understand all of His ways because we're not God. When we affirm that fact, our questions can become exclamations of worship. We don't understand, but God understands all things and is therefore worthy of praise.

PRAYER

Enter this time with your Bible and your heart open.
Based on the truths of Scripture, answer the following
questions and let them lead you to a time of prayer.

PRAISE

Contemplate your lack of understanding and God's limitless understanding.
Express praise to God that He's all-knowing, patient, and gracious to sinners.

REPENT

At any point has your questioning become impertinence before God? Repent
of any pride that has caused you to imply that God isn't handling His world
properly or that you could handle it better.

APPLY

When you see reports of sin and corruption in the world, use such moments
as opportunities to pray for the repentance of the people involved. Pray for
a just society. Pray that God will empower the church to arise, proclaim the
gospel, and work for good in the world.

YIELD

God's plan isn't your plan, His ways aren't your ways, and His timing isn't your
timing (see Isa. 55:8-9). But He's in charge of His world; you aren't. In prayer
submit to God and to His plan. Tell Him you want to fulfill His plan for your life.

In light of Scripture and based on your responses,
quiet yourself before the Lord and spend a few moments in prayer.

RECITING GOD'S ATTRIBUTES

> **Read Habakkuk 1:12–17.**

The Book of Habakkuk begins with Habakkuk's prayer in which he complained to God about all the wickedness in the world. God replied to Habakkuk, revealing to the prophet His plan to use the fierce, barbaric Babylonians to judge the sin of Judah. When Habakkuk heard God's plan, he responded by praying again.

In his second prayer Habakkuk recited the attributes of God's character, telling God that His plan conflicted with His character. Because God was the "Holy One" who executed judgment (v. 12), how could He be silent? Because God was pure and just, how could He "tolerate wrongdoing" (v. 13)?

Habakkuk was right to include in his prayer reminders of God's character. When we see injustice in the world or in our lives, concluding that God is unjust is easy but wrong. It's easy to base our feelings, thoughts, and decisions on our visible circumstances instead of on God's invisible character. However, God's character doesn't change, no matter what our circumstances may look like at the moment. It's unlikely that we'll move from doubting to worshiping if we don't embrace and profess that truth in prayer.

Habakkuk also used symbolic language to describe the idolatry of the Babylonians. They were taking joy in the fish they were catching instead of in the Creator of the fish (see vv. 14-15). They were worshiping their fishing nets instead of the one true God (see v. 16). Then Habakkuk asked God whether such idolaters would be allowed to enjoy prosperity from their fishing—victory over the nations they were slaughtering (see v. 17). With relentless honesty Habakkuk described to God what he observed and asked Him what He was going to do to intervene.

Habakkuk's list of God's attributes was orthodox but incomplete. He didn't include attributes like love, goodness, grace, and mercy. If Habakkuk had affirmed such attributes, perhaps he could have seen that God was refraining from His immediate judgment of the Babylonians because of His mercy. Perhaps Habakkuk could have also seen that at some point in the future, God would bless His faithful people because of His goodness and grace.

Habakkuk's profession of God's greatness in prayer gives us an example to follow. At every crossroads we recite God's attributes, remember that His character is unchanging, and wait for God to act according to His timing.

PRAYER

Enter this time with your Bible and your heart open.
Based on the truths of Scripture, answer the following
questions and let them lead you to a time of prayer.

PRAISE

Habakkuk praised God for His eternality, holiness, justice (see v. 12), purity
(see v. 13), and power in creation (see v. 14). How have you seen such divine
attributes in your experiences? Take time to praise God for these attributes,
plus others like grace, love, mercy, and goodness.

REPENT

When you remember God's holy attributes, how do you respond? Have you
questioned God's holiness, justice, or purity? Have you thought that His plan
or His ways are ill-advised? Have you thought that God should act more like
you? Confess such thoughts to God and ask His forgiveness for the presumption
of thinking you're capable of devising a plan that's better than His.

APPLY

Allow each circumstance in your daily life to stir you to praise God for one
of His holy attributes. Take time today to pray, remembering to recite God's
attributes that lead you to worship Him.

YIELD

Painful circumstances sometimes cause us to question or doubt God. Affirm
to God that He knows what you don't and can do what you can't. Tell Him that
you submit to Him and to His plan for your life, whatever that is.

In light of Scripture and based on your responses,
quiet yourself before the Lord and spend a few moments in prayer.

WHEN WE DON'T UNDERSTAND

Read Habakkuk 2.

In chapter 1 Habakkuk prayed, complaining to God about all the wickedness in the world. God answered Habakkuk, but the answer confused the prophet. Habakkuk asked God whether He was going to respond to wickedness with judgment.

Habakkuk 2 indicates what Habakkuk did next. He waited. In fact, he made a formal, poetic declaration of his intention to wait and see what God would say to him by way of explanation (see v. 1). Habakkuk used symbolic language to refer to his posture of waiting, portraying himself as a sentinel stationed on a tower. The job of such a guard was to scan the horizon for messengers or signs of danger approaching his city. On days or even weeks when nothing significant happened, waiting and watching must have become monotonous and boring. But when a courier brought important news or when an invading army approached, the sentinel could prove to be the most important person in the city.

Like a guard on a watchtower, Habakkuk was waiting and looking for the arrival of God's answers to his questions. Waiting isn't easy, but in a relationship with God, waiting is inevitable and therefore an essential discipline. We wait on God for answers; we wait on God for direction; and after we think we know what God wants us to do, we wait for the right time to implement His will.

Waiting on God has a long history. God wants us to wait on Him so that we'll learn to depend on Him. Because He's God, He was under no obligation to answer Habakkuk, but He did. He told Habakkuk that He would judge wicked Babylon after He used that nation to judge wicked Judah. God gave His prophet a dramatic description of proud Babylon's fall. He declared five woes over Babylon, announcing that its sin would result in its suffering. In the end God would vindicate right and punish wrong, exercising His holy sovereignty over all things. In the meantime His faithful people waited.

PRAYER

Enter this time with your Bible and your heart open.
Based on the truths of Scripture, answer the following
questions and let them lead you to a time of prayer.

PRAISE

Praise God for seeing you when you're waiting on Him. Praise God for answering your prayers according to His good purpose and in His perfect timing. He assures you that one day the earth will be filled with the knowledge of the Lord (2:14).

REPENT

Have you been unwilling to wait on God? Does your unwillingness to wait signal a lack of dependence on God? Has God's present silence caused you to doubt God or to confuse His present work with His final work?

APPLY

Habakkuk 2:20 says:

> The LORD is in his holy temple;
> let the whole earth
> be silent in his presence.
> **HABAKKUK 2:20**

Enter God's presence, tell Him your needs and questions, and wait in humble silence before Him. Conclude your time of silence in God's presence by asking Him to use you to help bring everyone on earth to faith in the one true God.

YIELD

Meditate on the fact that God is sovereign over all nations and all people. He works His holy will in all situations according to His good pleasure. Confess to God in prayer that He's also in charge of your life. Submit to Him and His plan for you. Tell Him that you're dependent on Him.

In light of Scripture and based on your responses,
quiet yourself before the Lord and spend a few moments in prayer.

LIVING BY FAITH

Read Habakkuk 2:1-4.

Habakkuk observed the wickedness in his country, grieved over it, and asked God what He was going to do about the evil in the world. God answered Habakkuk by telling him that He was going to use Babylon to punish Judah. That word confused Habakkuk, because Babylon was even more wicked than Judah. Habakkuk waited on God for an explanation, and eventually God revealed to him that He would punish Babylon in His time and that His righteous plan would win in the end.

Before God revealed His plan for the future to Habakkuk, He gave His prophet instructions on what to do with His revelation—He told him to write it down (v. 4). Habakkuk had been like a sentinel on a wall waiting for God's answer to arrive. God told him to transition to the role of a writer. Habakkuk was to record God's message so that everyone could read it, because God's revelation was important and public.

God began His message with a contrast between the ungodly and the righteous. The ungodly (the Babylonians) were "inflated" and "without integrity" (v. 4). In other words, they were puffed up and not upright. The ungodly exalt themselves, not God, and they walk in their own ways, not God's.

The second part of verse 4 is a mountain peak of revelation in the Old Testament: "The righteous one will live by his faith." This verse is quoted three times in the New Testament (see Rom. 1:17; Gal. 3:11; Heb. 10:38). Why is this statement so important?

- Habakkuk 2:4 communicates that God gives us spiritual life, eternal life, on the basis of our faith, not our works (see Rom. 1:16-17; Gal. 3:9-11). We can't earn right standing with God by our good works. God grants such salvation on the basis of our faith in Him (see Gen. 15:6).
- Habakkuk 2:4 means we live each day by faith, or trust in God. Habakkuk had to wait on God to answer his questions. Because he was waiting on God, he was trusting in God, not in himself. In the same way, we're to live by faith, not by our sight. Often we can't see God's plan. We're to live by faith, not by our understanding. Our understanding is limited, but God's knowledge is unlimited. We're to live by faith, not by our strength. Our strength often falls short. God's power never fails, so we put our faith in Him. And such living faith always results in faithfulness—walking in God's ways (see Jas. 2:17-26).

PRAYER

*Enter this time with your Bible and your heart open.
Based on the truths of Scripture, answer the following
questions and let them lead you to a time of prayer.*

PRAISE

As God revealed His future plans to Habakkuk, He reveals His truth to you through His Word, the Bible. The divine inspiration of the Scriptures is a miracle. Give God praise for His greatness and grace in revealing His truth to you. Also tell Him that He's worthy of your trust at all times.

REPENT

In what ways have you trusted yourself instead of God? Repent for trusting in anything or anyone other than God. Has your faith resulted in faithful living? Repent of any evidence of a lack of faithfulness.

APPLY

Just as God gave Habakkuk a message to share, God's Word directs followers of Jesus to share the gospel with all nations. Think about a few individuals or people groups. Pray for them and plan ways you can share the gospel with them

YIELD

Have you been living daily by trusting in your own strength and knowledge instead of living by faith in God? Tell God you'll trust Him today, not yourself.

*In light of Scripture and based on your responses,
quiet yourself before the Lord and spend a few moments in prayer.*

UNCONDITIONAL FAITH

Read Habakkuk 3.

Habakkuk began his final hymn with a lengthy expression of praise and faith that declared the state of his heart. He stood in awe of God and desired to see Him renew His work in the prophet's lifetime (see v. 2). Next, perhaps overcome by the extended description of God's judgment of Babylon in chapter 2, Habakkuk implored God, "In your wrath remember mercy!" (v. 2).

Habakkuk then launched into a lengthy symbolic description of God's greatness. He portrayed God as arriving in Judah from neighboring Edom (Teman and Mount Paran, v. 3). But God's greatness far exceeded such geographical boundaries: "His splendor covers the heavens" (v. 3). Just as God is great, He's also holy and won't allow evil to triumph. In response Habakkuk wrote statements like these:

> Plague goes before Him.
> You crush the leader of the house of the wicked.
> **HABAKKUK 3:5,13**

Habakkuk concluded his book with a beautiful expression of unconditional faith:

> Though the fig tree does not bud
> and there is no fruit on the vines, ...
> yet I will celebrate in the LORD;
> I will rejoice in the God of my salvation!
> **HABAKKUK 3:17-18**

In other words, no matter what happened to Habakkuk—whether or not his faith resulted in blessing, whether or not he understood what God was doing—he still intended to trust in God.

We'll never completely understand God, because He's God. We won't always understand His ways or the circumstances and trials He allows to enter our lives. Will we trust, love, and praise Him anyway? "The righteous one will live by his faith" (2:4).

PRAYER

Enter this time with your Bible and your heart open.
Based on the truths of Scripture, answer the following
questions and let them lead you to a time of prayer.

PRAISE

Habakkuk provided a poetic, pictorial portrayal of God's greatness (see 3:3-15). As you read that depiction again, "stand in awe" of God (v. 2) and tremble over His glory (see v. 16).

REPENT

Habakkuk 3 vividly describes God's resolute opposition to sin. He opposes sin in your life too. Ask God to reveal individual sins in your heart. Confess and repent of each one.

APPLY

Tell someone today that you're rejoicing in the God of your salvation (see v. 18). Because God is your strength and enables you (see v. 19), tell Him today that you want to live by His strength instead of yours. Ask Him to fill you with His Holy Spirit.

YIELD

Have you trusted God more when life was going well and less when life was going badly? Reject such conditional faith and tell God that you'll trust Him no matter what happens.

In light of Scripture and based on your responses,
quiet yourself before the Lord and spend a few moments in prayer.

WEEK 10

The Prayer of Jonah

START

Welcome to group session 10 of *Praying at the Crossroads.*

Use the following questions to begin the session.

Session 10 brings us to the story and the prayer of Jonah. His brief prayer has much to offer us today in terms of its beauty, substance, and example. This week's study will consider several different aspects of Jonah's prayer that can strengthen and deepen the prayers of God's people.

What comes to mind when you think about the story of Jonah?

Why do people turn to prayer at the end of their rope?

Jonah was one of the four writing prophets of the Bible whom Jesus mentioned by name (the others were Isaiah, Daniel, and Zechariah). However, Jesus spoke of Jonah in a unique way, observing that Jonah's three days in the belly of the great fish foreshadowed His own death and resurrection. Jesus said, "As Jonah was in the belly of the huge fish three days and three nights, so the Son of Man will be in the heart of the earth three days and three nights" (Matt. 12:40).

From the belly of the fish, Jonah cried out to the Lord in humility, despair, and brokenness, acknowledging that this discipline came from the Lord and that God was right in his actions. He also acknowledged that deliverance and salvation ultimately come from Almighty God. We see from Jonah's story that our God hears our prayers, corrects and restores sinners, and provides second chances for people who turn to Him.

Use these statements to follow along as you watch video session 10.

Jonah wanted to do things his own way.

In the belly of the great fish, Jonah cried out to the Lord.

Jonah's prayer speaks to us about the sovereignty of God.

Application from Jonah's Prayer

1. Jonah said he was afflicted by the Lord and felt the discipline and the heavy hand of God.

2. Jonah described a time of deep despair.

3. Jonah returned to the Lord.

4. Jonah called out to God in thanksgiving.

5. Jonah was well acquainted with the Word of God.

God loves us too much for us to get away with rebellion or apathy toward God.

As we pray, may we acknowledge God's sovereignty and that God is working circumstances in our lives so that we would walk in obedience, that we would be shaped into the likeness of His Son, Jesus Christ.

Oftentimes God uses times of despair when we have our deepest level of prayer, when we cry out to the Lord.

God hears our prayers when we pray in His will.

A spirit of gratitude in our prayer lives postures our heart before God in a beautiful way.

Pray through the promises and the power and the very Word of God.

Video sessions available at lifeway.com/prayingatthecrossroads
or with a subscription to smallgroup.com

DISCUSS

Use the following questions to discuss the video teaching.

Read Jonah 1–2.

Jonah's story took place around 750 BC. As a prophet, Jonah, was called to speak to the people of Israel on God's behalf. When God told Jonah to go outside Israel and speak to the people of Nineveh, the capital city of Assyria, he refused and fled in the opposite direction.

No doubt Jonah knew the people of Assyria were enemies of Israel, renowned for their cruel, vicious atrocities against humanity, including the people of Israel. Jonah simply didn't like them and didn't want to go, despite what God said. The climax of the story came when the prodigal prophet was swallowed by a great fish, which God had appointed for this special purpose. It's from the belly of the fish that Jonah offered his prayer.

When has God supernaturally worked in your life to get your attention?

What work of God have you have ignored, causing Him to use more extraordinary means to get your attention?

As a result of his rebellion and disobedience, Jonah found himself in a difficult situation. Clearly, if Jonah had simply obeyed God, no storm and no great fish would have been required to bring about Jonah's hardship and feelings of despair. Yet as sinful people, we all sometimes find ourselves under the loving chastisement of our sovereign God. Often our sin is outright rebellion against God's will. At other times our sin is just apathy about God's purposes. Whatever the case may be, God loves us too much to let us squander our lives in apathy or disobedience. Such was the case with the prophet Jonah.

Have you ever thought about apathy as sinful? Why or why not? Why should we think about it this way?

When has the Lord allowed or brought about a storm in your life for the purpose of teaching and correction? How did this experience change your life and bring about the sweet fruit of divine discipline?

In times like these it's vital to remember that God loves us and that ultimately, "All things work together for the good of those who love God, who are called according to his purpose" (Rom. 8:28). We mustn't lose sight of God's ultimate purpose for us to become more holy and Christlike. A healthy prayer life keeps us tethered to the Lord in the midst of storms that help teach, correct, grow, and conform us to the image and likeness of Jesus.

Jesus taught us:

> Ask, and it will be given to you. Seek, and you will find. Knock, and the door will be opened to you. For everyone who asks receives, and the one who seeks finds, and to the one who knocks, the door will be opened. Who among you, if his son asks him for bread, will give him a stone? Or if he asks for a fish, will give him a snake? If you then, who are evil, know how to give good gifts to your children, how much more will your Father in heaven give good things to those who ask him.
> **MATTHEW 7:7–11**

How earnestly do you seek the Lord in prayer? How are you actively asking, seeking, and knocking as the Lord instructs?

Why should we seek the Lord before storms and troubles come?

Do you lack wisdom? We all do. God wants you to seek Him for answers and promises:

> If any of you lacks wisdom, he should ask God—who gives to all generously and ungrudgingly—and it will be given to him.
> **JAMES 1:5**

When you ask for wisdom, God will abundantly help you without finding fault. How amazing our God is!

When was the most recent time you asked God for understanding in a particular situation?

GROUP PRAYER

Use the following PRAY framework to pray together as a group.

In light of what we've studied today, pray together as a group, using the following prompts to guide your experience together. You'll repeat this exercise at the end of each day's personal study. Use the biblical prayer we studied to guide your own. Read each prompt aloud and encourage group members to lift up prayers based on these prompts silently or aloud, depending on their comfort level.

PRAISE *God for who He is and what He has done.*

Move beyond praising God just for material and temporary things. Praise Him for blessings of greater, eternal value. Praise God for sending His Son, Jesus, so that our sins could be forgiven and we could obtain eternal life through faith in His life, death, and resurrection.

REPENT *of unconfessed sins and accept Christ's forgiveness.*

Like Jonah, we all have a clear word from the Lord. God has revealed Himself to us in the Scriptures. Any failure to follow God's commands in His Word is sin you need to repent of. Examine your heart and ask God to forgive you.

APPLY *the truths you've learned by committing to action.*

One beautiful aspect of Jonah's prayer is his open transparency with God. Jonah prayed naturally, vulnerably, respectfully, honestly, and relationally. Let's follow his example by praying as a child to a loving Father who deeply loves and cares for us.

YIELD *your life to God's will and kind providence.*

Jonah genuinely called out to God in humility and brokenness, recognizing that only God could deliver him. Let's also recognize that God is our helper who'll never leave or forsake us (see Heb. 13:5-6). Let's pray to our God and find help, comfort, assurance, peace, and joy in all situations in our lives.

Close by praying for specific requests that arose during the session.

PRAY, KNOWING GOD'S SOVEREIGNTY

Read Jonah 1:1-3.

Understanding and embracing God's sovereignty will greatly affect the depth and confidence of our prayers. Knowing that our God is all-powerful, all-knowing, all-present, and all-loving gives us great boldness when we pray. In fact, praying to a god who isn't sovereign would seem counterproductive and even futile.

In the Old Testament God's people called out to Him in prayer, having full assurance in His sovereign ability. In the Book of Job, Job said:

> I know that you can do anything
> and no plan of yours can be thwarted.
> **JOB 42:2**

How wonderfully reassuring it is to know with complete certainty that our God is good and is able to do all things according to His good and perfect will.

The Book of Jonah sets forth both God's sovereignty and His ability to hear the prayers of His people. Even though Jonah was rebelling against God, he could clearly see God's sovereign hand controlling the events in his life.

In Jonah 1:2 we read that God told Jonah to go to Nineveh. After all, God is the boss. When Jonah refused, God summoned a storm to severely rattle the ship, for even the weather is at God's command. When Jonah was tossed overboard, God appointed a great fish to come and swallow him and eventually to spit him up at the appointed place.

God wasn't going to allow Jonah to get away with his rebellion. Although God's stance didn't please Jonah at the time, it clearly pictures God's sovereign ability to retrieve a wayward child. Ultimately, Jonah realized that the best response to the sovereign God was to walk in obedience to Him, so he cried out to God in prayer for a miraculous deliverance.

Scripture reveals a God who cares for His people. He offers love, protection, blessing, and the blessings a loving Father wants for His children. He even encourages us to come boldly into His presence and to make our requests known to Him (see Phil. 4:6; Heb. 4:16). In our study of Jonah's prayer, we'll see that each event works together for the good of God's people and for the glory of God.

PRAYER

Enter this time with your Bible and your heart open.
Based on the truths of Scripture, answer the following
questions and let them lead you to a time of prayer.

PRAISE

Praise the Lord and express your gratitude that He's completely sovereign
and in control of all things. Praise Him for the way He orchestrates the details
of your life. Rejoice that God is working all things together for your good (see
Rom. 8:28). Express gratitude for His sovereign care and provision for you.

REPENT

Faith is having confidence in God's Word and believing what God says:
"Without faith it is impossible to please God, since the one who draws near
to him must believe that he exists and that he rewards those who seek him"
(Heb. 11:6). Do you approach God in prayer, knowing He's able to do more
than you could ask or imagine? Has your prayer life suffered because you
haven't trusted God enough to ask Him in prayer?

APPLY

Once you understand and embrace God's sovereignty, you should be encouraged
to pray more frequently and with utmost confidence. Praise and express
gratitude to Him for all of His amazing attributes.

YIELD

God's ways are better than our ways. In prayer submit to God and to His plan
for your life. Tell God that you want to fulfill His plans and purpose for your
life as your first priority.

In light of Scripture and based on your responses,
quiet yourself before the Lord and spend a few moments in prayer.

STORMS THAT COMPEL US TO PRAY

> Read Jonah 1:4–2:2.

Sometimes we become complacent or even rebellious toward the Lord. In these times God often uses difficulties and hardships to bring us back into a right and even deeper relationship with Himself. These storms drive us to prayer. This was certainly the case with Jonah.

The Book of Jonah begins with Jonah fleeing from the Lord on a ship. God responded to Jonah's disobedience by bringing a literal storm into his life (see 1:4-5). Jonah's situation went from bad to worse, for when he was tossed overboard …

> The LORD appointed a great fish to swallow Jonah, and Jonah
> was in the belly of the fish three days and three nights.
> **JONAH 1:17**

God works all things for good in the lives of His people (see Rom. 8:28), even in sending storms. As we move into chapter 2, we see that God's purpose in sending this storm was being realized. The prodigal prophet was now crying out to God rather than running from Him.

God still works this way in the lives of His people. He has a perfect, effective way of capturing our attention. As a pastor, I frequently observe people who are coasting though life with everything seeming to go their way. In their comfort they're less likely to pay attention in worship services and generally less interested in prayer. In contrast, members who are experiencing difficulty pay close attention during the sermon, have a sweet brokenness about them, and rarely miss an opportunity to pray. The psalmist Asaph recorded the same sentiment: "I sought the Lord in my day of trouble" (Ps. 77:2). The Lord's love for His children compels Him to send storms into our lives so that we'll seek Him. King David wrote:

> It was good for me to be afflicted
> so that I could learn your statutes.
> **PSALM 119:71**

PRAYER

Enter this time with your Bible and your heart open.
Based on the truths of Scripture, answer the following
questions and let them lead you to a time of prayer.

PRAISE

Two boys were complaining because their fathers spanked them for disobedience. Another boy heard their complaints and replied, "I wish my dad cared enough about me to spank me." Praise and thank God for His amazing love, which compels Him to discipline you for your benefit and holiness.

REPENT

A response in prayer and obedience is God's desire. In prayer turn from pride and rebellion and listen to what God is trying to teach you.

APPLY

Understanding the way God interacts with you as His child is vital to your spiritual well-being and growth. During storms from God, be quick to pray, repent, and learn the purpose God is trying to teach you.

YIELD

It took Jonah a little while to surrender his prideful rebellion. Be quick to yield and surrender to what the Lord is trying to accomplish. Allow God to shape, correct, and form you more and more into the likeness of Jesus through these storms of life.

In light of Scripture and based on your responses,
quiet yourself before the Lord and spend a few moments in prayer.

DEEP DESPAIR, DEEPER PRAYER

Read Jonah 2:1-6.

In Jonah 2 we find the prodigal prophet in deep despair. The Lord had afflicted Jonah by sending a great storm to the ship on which he was attempting to escape. Through a series of events, the crew had cast Jonah overboard, and he was swallowed by a great fish that God had appointed for the occasion. Jonah's prayer in chapter 2 makes it abundantly clear that he was experiencing agonizing despair.

Today God's people can also find themselves in despair arising from illness, financial turmoil, difficulty with children, conflict with parents, abuse, marital issues, or other trials. In times of despair we may even feel that God has abandoned us.

Jonah's prayer sets forth an example of hope. Jonah cried out to God from a deep, dark place, and God met him there. The Lord heard Jonah and answered him. In the depths of despair, Jonah stopped running from God and started crying out to God. This response is what God wanted before Jonah ever boarded the ship. God wants our attention. He's jealous for us, not willing to sit by and watch our hearts be drawn away by affections for the things of this world.

Jonah's prayer made the difference as he lifted his voice and his eyes toward heaven. God answered Jonah and brought his life up from the pit. Jonah was able to look to God and rejoice in His salvation with a heart of gratitude.

In times of deep anguish, people turn either to God or away from God. Often those who turn to the Lord in the midst of despair are rewarded with more intimate closeness to God. The Lord allows these times of deep despair to draw us into His presence, to strengthen our dependency on Him, and to help us realize what truly matters.

PRAYER

Enter this time with your Bible and your heart open.
Based on the truths of Scripture, answer the following
questions and let them lead you to a time of prayer.

PRAISE

God is worthy of your praise simply for who He is. Yet this passage of Scripture reminds you to praise Him because He promises, "I will never leave you or abandon you" (Heb. 13:5). Although Jonah was running away from God in disobedience, God was there to deliver Him from the pit.

REPENT

Have you responded to God with anger or resentment about hardships in your life? Turn from an attitude that seeks to blame God and trust in God's goodness toward you: "All things work together for the good of those who love God, who are called according to his purpose" (Rom. 8:28).

APPLY

Believe that God is attempting to teach you, correct you, draw you closer to Himself, and ultimately shape and conform you into the image and likeness of His Son.

YIELD

Because God is gracious, merciful, kind, loving, compassionate, all-powerful, all-knowing, and all-present, you can trust in Him today.

In light of Scripture and based on your responses,
quiet yourself before the Lord and spend a few moments in prayer.

SECOND CHANCES

Read Jonah 2:7–3:3.

Remembering the various attributes of God is an effective way to increase the quality and depth of our prayers. Praising and thanking the Lord for His grace, mercy, faithfulness, and steadfast love blesses us, especially as we consider how frequently we fail Him. In our prayers we should express genuine gratitude that the Lord is patient and long-suffering toward His children, remembering that He forgives sin and restores stumbling believers who haven't always followed His will and His Word. Praise Him, for He's the God of second chances. Praise Him, for He hears our prayers.

A major theme in the Book of Jonah is Jonah's repentance and restoration. Jonah cried out to the Lord and humbled himself before God in his prayer. Jonah expressed his willingness to obey, and God heard his prayer. God responded by giving Jonah a second chance: "The LORD commanded the fish, and it vomited Jonah onto dry land" (Jonah 2:10).

The first time God instructed Jonah to go to Nineveh, Jonah refused and went in the opposite direction. Now, as a result of God's affliction, Jonah prayed, and God responded to his prayer. The second time God instructed Jonah to go to Nineveh, Jonah obeyed, and we see the sweet fruit of repentance that leads to obedience:

> The word of the LORD came to Jonah a second time: "Get up! Go to
> the great city of Nineveh and preach the message that I tell you."
> Jonah got up and went to Nineveh according to the LORD's command.
> **JONAH 3:1-3**

Thank You, Lord, for hearing our prayers and giving us a second chance. To be sure, God's ways are higher than our ways (see Isa. 55:9). He works in our lives to bring about repentance and prayer so that we'll walk in obedience. Never be afraid to tell God you're sorry for your sin and to ask for a second chance to fulfill the privileged work He has for you. Remember that Jonah's repentant prayer was answered, Jonah was restored, and God was glorified.

PRAYER

Enter this time with your Bible and your heart open.
Based on the truths of Scripture, answer the following
questions and let them lead you to a time of prayer.

PRAISE

Jonah set a great example of praising God in prayer. He expressed that the Lord is worthy of thanksgiving and sacrifice, and he praised the Lord for His gift of salvation. Why should we continually thank God for our salvation?

REPENT

God gives us the gift of repentance. When we hit rock bottom, we realize that He's the rock. What confidence does it give you in repentance and confession to know that God is always there and ready to receive you?

APPLY

Consider the brokenness and genuineness of Jonah's heartfelt prayer. Thank God for the grace, mercy, love, and patience He has extended to you. Praise the Lord for the second chances He has given to you.

YIELD

How do you respond in dark times? Trouble surrounds you, and life seems hopeless. Let God speak into your life. Look for the God-given second chance. Resist the temptation to indulge in self-pity. Instead, use your difficult circumstance as an opportunity to get right with God.

In light of Scripture and based on your responses,
quiet yourself before the Lord and spend a few moments in prayer.

SCRIPTURE-RICH PRAYERS

Read Matthew 6:9–13.

To conclude this week's study, let's consider something of great value in Jonah's prayer. Though it may not be readily obvious, there's a treasure for us to discover. Jonah's prayer contains something very special: God's Word. According to Warren Wiersbe, Jonah's prayer, though only ten verses, "is composed of quotations from at least fifteen different psalms."[1] This little prayer demonstrates that Jonah spent time in God's Word. He understood the character, the power, and the promises of God. In fact, Jonah's knowledge of God's Word serves as the foundation of his prayer.

God's people would greatly benefit from praying Scripture-rich prayers for every need, every hardship, every trial, and every aspect of our lives. Praying God's promises and the truths found in the Bible provides a great guide as we pray for family, friends, leaders, missionaries, and circumstances. Incorporating God's Word into our prayers is rewarding and fruitful, reminding us of God's faithfulness and trustworthy character.

Praying Scripture-rich prayers is a valuable discipline for believers of any age or level of Christian maturity. The Lord Himself gave us a guide for prayer when He taught His disciples to pray like this:

Our Father in heaven,
your name be honored as holy.
Your kingdom come.
Your will be done
on earth as it is in heaven.
Give us today our daily bread.
And forgive us our debts,
as we also have forgiven our debtors.
And do not bring us into temptation,
but deliver us from the evil one.
MATTHEW 6:9–13

PRAYER

Enter this time with your Bible and your heart open.
Based on the truths of Scripture, answer the following
questions and let them lead you to a time of prayer.

PRAISE

Praise the Lord for two of His wonderful gifts, the Scriptures and the gift of prayer. Thank Him for making Himself available 24/7. Give thanks for revealing Himself to you through the living Word and the written Word.

REPENT

Do your prayers lack depth and understanding of God's will? Are your prayers often misguided and confused? Are your prayers inconsistent with sound doctrine? Praying God's Word can guide and strengthen your prayers.

APPLY

Have you ever prayed Scripture-rich prayers? Have you ever prayed the prayers of the Bible? Praying God's Word involves a commitment to study the Scriptures and the discipline to incorporate them into your prayers. You'll find the effort to be fruitful and rewarding.

YIELD

Where are some other place in God's Word we find God's people praying? How can you incorporate those prayers into your own prayer?

In light of Scripture and based on your responses,
quiet yourself before the Lord and spend a few moments in prayer.

START

Welcome to group session 11 of *Praying at the Crossroads*.

Use the following questions to begin the session.

How often do you confess your sins? When was the most recent time, and what was your motive in doing so? How would you describe those prayers?

Have you ever gossiped about the mistakes and sins of other people? Did you ever think to pray on their behalf?

The seventeenth-century Puritan John Owen said, "What that minister is on his knees in secret before God Almighty, that he is and no more."[1] If Owen is right, then Daniel was quite a man. That's certainly what God thought. The angel Gabriel said to Daniel, "You are treasured by God" (Dan 9:23). The English Standard Version translates this verse, "You are greatly loved."

In Daniel 9:4-19 Daniel prayed a remarkable prayer that contained both corporate confession of sin and recognition of God's greatness. God's man confessed and interceded for God's sinful people. Daniel's prayer is a model for the way God's people should pray.

The brokenness and humility of Daniel as he prayed for "all Israel" (v. 7) are amazing. Yet we shouldn't be surprised. As Charles Spurgeon said:

> A True-Hearted believer does not live for himself. Where there is abundance of grace, a great strength of mind in the service of God, there is sure to be a spirit of unselfishness. ... Daniel's prayer should, by the blessing of God's Spirit, inspire us with the spirit of prayer; and that his example, in forgetting himself, and remembering his people, should help us to be unselfish, and lead us to care for our people—even God's people—to whom we have the honor and privilege to belong.[2]

As we study the prayer of Daniel, we'll ask God to make us men and women of prayer like him.[3]

Use these statements to follow along as you watch video session 11.

Daniel was placed in the lion's den because he was a man of prayer.

Daniel 9 is not primarily directed to a nation as a whole. Daniel 9 is directed to the people of God.

Daniel's prayer is rich both in terms of its theology and as a model for us to adopt.

Daniel's Prayer
1. Saturated with Scripture   2. Brutally honest   3. Humble   4. Corporate

Daniel knew the Word of God so well, he could actually pray the Word of God back to our Lord.

Why God's Judgment Was Just
- Sinned, done wrong, acted wickedly, rebelled, turned aside (v. 5)
- Have not listened to You (v. 6)
- Because of our treachery (v. 7)
- Have sinned (v. 8)
- Have rebelled (v. 9)
- Have not obeyed (v. 10)
- Transgressed Your law, turned aside, refused to obey Your voice, have sinned (v. 11)
- Guilty of iniquity (v. 13)
- Have not obeyed Your voice (v. 14)
- Have sinned and done wickedly (v. 15)
- Our sins, the iniquities of our fathers (v. 16)

Daniel honestly acknowledged before the Lord, "We have no excuse. What we have received in terms of Your judgment, we have deserved."

There is a sense in which the Bible clearly affirms the solidarity and the corporate nature of God's people.

Video sessions available at lifeway.com/prayingatthecrossroads or with a subscription to smallgroup.com

DISCUSS

Use the following questions to discuss the video teaching.

Most of the time people don't talk about their moral failures. Anger, theft, and sinful thoughts aren't the type of details you post online about yourself. You don't mention them in job interviews. However, when Daniel prayed, he put his sin and the sin of Israel on full display. He confessed all of the ways they had done wrong. He didn't hide their sins or try to reason his way out of responsibility. He confessed all of their sins directly, truthfully, and humbly. His prayer in Daniel 9:4-19 reminds us that God is serious about our sin. It reminds us that we're to bring our sin to God without trying to hide it or minimize it. It also reminds us that He's ready to forgive.

How can pride and arrogance ruin your prayers?

What are some ways the Scriptures can shape your prayers?

When Daniel saw the sin of his people, he was overwhelmed. He knew God's people weren't enjoying the life God wanted because they had rejected God and hadn't obeyed Him. Daniel's heart ached for them to have a renewed relationship with God. Prayers in the Bible don't mask feelings. They often exhibit sadness, burdens, and heartache. Daniel wore sackcloth and ashes to display his emotions and his commitment to repent before God.

Daniel prayed with a great burden on his heart. What burdens do you need to give to God? Why should you always feel comfortable doing this?

If God knows all things, why is it important for us to confess our sins to God?

Daniel identified himself with the sinful people of Israel. How should you respond to and relate to the sins of other Christians?

Daniel prayed that God would forgive and restore His people. He prayed that God would be faithful to His promises. He didn't pray on the basis of his goodness or of his intention to do something for God. He didn't come with selfish motives, thinking he could use God to get something else. Because he knew Scripture, he knew God's character and promises. He also knew his own character in comparison to God's. Knowing that God was committed to His people, Daniel prayed that God would keep His promises.

> *Do you avoid full confession of your sin to God? What are some common ways you do this?*

> *How can God be merciful and forgiving if He's holy and must punish sin?*

> *How does Daniel's prayer point to the gospel and to what Christ has done for you?*

When we pray to God, we can confess our sins instead of hiding them. When we've done wrong, we don't have to hide our sin. We don't have to fear God will reject us. We can admit wrongdoing because we know God is kind and merciful. Daniel prayed and confessed because he believed God had abundant compassion. He believed God loved His people and would forgive them.

GROUP PRAYER

Use the following PRAY framework to pray together as a group.

In light of what we've studied today, pray together as a group, using the following prompts to guide your experience together. You'll repeat this exercise at the end of each day's personal study. Use the biblical prayer we studied to guide your own. Read each prompt aloud and encourage group members to lift up prayers based on these prompts silently or aloud, depending on their comfort level.

PRAISE *God for who He is and what He has done.*

Just as God was merciful and ready to forgive Israel of its sins, He's ready to forgive our sins today. Praise God that He patiently waits for us to repent and always welcomes us back when we return to Him.

REPENT *of unconfessed sins and accept Christ's forgiveness.*

Daniel knew his personal sins and the sins of all Israel mattered to God. Confess the ways you've sinned individually and as part of a group (for example, marriage, family, church, school, or work).

APPLY *the truths you've learned by committing to action.*

The Lord gave His commands so that we could have full joy and life in Him. Forgiveness means we can't work to gain God's pleasure, but we're set free to obey with the proper motivation. Pray that God will show you ways you need to obey Him.

YIELD *your life to God's will and kind providence.*

Because God sees everyone's sin and because we're accountable to Him for every word and action, yield your life to Him by repenting of your sin and by expressing your desire to obey Him.

Close by praying for specific requests that arose during the session.

PRAYER FLOWING FROM THE SCRIPTURES

Read Daniel 9:1–2.

Daniel 9:1 says it was the first year of Darius the Mede (another name or title for Cyrus; see 5:31; 6:1). The year was around 538 BC, shortly before legend says a Greek soldier would run the world's first marathon. This date was approximately twelve years after Daniel's vision of the ram and the goat in chapter 8. Daniel was now more than eighty years old. Having outlived the Babylonian Empire, he now served under Medo-Persia.

Daniel was reading the Bible, "the books according to the word of the LORD" (9:2). Specifically, he was reading in the prophet Jeremiah "that the number of years for the desolation of Jerusalem would be seventy" (v. 2). This predictive promise is found in Jeremiah 25:1-14; 29:1-11. Israel had sinned by worshiping idols, so God had judged the nation as He promised He would by sending it into exile in Babylon. Jeremiah had revealed that this exile would last seventy years. Daniel was exiled with others in 605 BC, and it was now 538 BC. Daniel knew the period of God's judgment was coming to an end. And he knew Yahweh was a covenant God who kept His Word: "What Scripture says is what God says, and what God says happens."[4]

When God makes a promise in His Word, it will come to pass just as He says it will. Daniel read and meditated on Scripture and trusted it as a reliable Word from God. Exiled, captive in a godless land, and rapidly moving toward the end of his life, Daniel still had great hope for his people in light of the certain promises of God's Word. Confidence in God's promises didn't move Daniel to complacency. It drove him to his knees and to action.

God delights in the prayers of His children that emerge from time spent in His Word: "Only as we deepen our understanding of God as revealed in the Bible will our praying become richer and more soundly based on who God is."[5] God has given us His Word so that we can know Him and speak with Him.

PRAYER

Enter this time with your Bible and your heart open.
Based on the truths of Scripture, answer the following
questions and let them lead you to a time of prayer.

PRAISE

Daniel knew God would keep His promise to restore Israel. Where else
in Scripture do you see God keeping His promises? What promises has
God given in His Word for you and your life?

REPENT

Israel often didn't believe God would keep His Word. How have you failed
to trust that God will do what He says?

APPLY

Daniel knew God's promises because he knew Scripture. Many Christians
find that it's more difficult to pray when they don't spend time in God's Word.
Why do you think that's true? Do you find it to be true in your life?

YIELD

The world often offers counterfeit gifts that tempt you not to desire God's
promises. What would it look like in your life this week to trust in God's
promises instead of what the world offers?

In light of Scripture and based on your responses,
quiet yourself before the Lord and spend a few moments in prayer.

HUMBLY TAKEN INTO THE PRESENCE OF GOD

Read Daniel 9:3-4.

Daniel 9:3 reveals the humble, contrite attitude with which Daniel approached "the Lord God" in prayer. He began by turning from his reading of the Scriptures to the face of "the LORD my God" (v. 4). A deep earnestness in Daniel's heart moved him to look to his Lord. Seeking the Lord "by prayer and pleas for mercy" (v. 3, ESV), he approached Him in the threefold posture of "fasting, sackcloth, and ashes" (v. 3). Some of these practices are foreign to us, but David Helm explains:

> Fasting is the withholding of food from the body for the sake
> of prioritizing something else, such as prayer. Sackcloth
> was a rough material, most likely made from animal skins
> that would have been an irritant to the skin, and was a mark
> of repentance. Ashes symbolized complete ruin. In other
> words, the posture of Daniel took was of visible lament.[6]

Daniel turned to the Lord with a heavy heart, a burden he could hardly bear. His prayer should remind us of a prayer offered in a garden called Gethsemane around six hundred years later. In Gethsemane our Lord Jesus turned His face to His Father in humble pleas for mercy (see Luke 22:39-46). The burden of bearing the sins of the world (see John 1:29) caused "his sweat [to become] like drops of blood falling to the ground" (Luke 24:44). When Jesus humbly and dependently came into the presence of His Father, His prayer was heard: "Not my will, but yours, be done" (v. 42). His Father gave Him strength to endure the cross that lay ahead.

Jesus humbled Himself both to pray and to prepare for His passion. It's truly unconscionable to think we would burst into God's presence in arrogance or pride. When we know our sin and the sins of our people, we'll approach God on our knees and with our face to the ground. Only then can we turn our face to the Lord with our prayers and pleas. Only then can we rightly pour out our heart and soul to "the LORD my God" (Dan. 9:4).

PRAYER

Enter this time with your Bible and your heart open.
Based on the truths of Scripture, answer the following
questions and let them lead you to a time of prayer.

PRAISE

Daniel knew that even though Israel had rebelled, God would still hear
his prayers if he came to Him humbly. Why does God continue to listen
to the prayers of people who've sinned?

REPENT

When you sinned, do you run from God, or do you run to Him in prayer?
Are you humble or arrogant? Can you trust that God will listen to you
if you come to Him arrogantly? Why or why not?

APPLY

Daniel not only pray but also fasted and wore sackcloth and ashes. Why did
he feel that these disciplines were necessary? How can you use your outward
posture to approach God humbly?

YIELD

Are you concerned about both your sin and the sins of others? Are you more
eager to gossip or to pray when you hear about someone else's sin? How can
you make sure it's the latter?

In light of Scripture and based on your responses,
quiet yourself before the Lord and spend a few moments in prayer.

HONEST, FULL CONFESSION OF SIN

Read Daniel 9:4-14.

The prayer of Daniel, which appears in Daniel 9:4-19, is characterized by two major themes: corporate confession of sin and acknowledgment of God's character and mighty acts of salvation. As Daniel piled up terms to describe Israel and Judah's sin, he used the word *we, us,* or *our* more than twenty times. He was identifying with the people's sin. Bryan Chapell writes:

> Daniel confesses the reality of his sin and the people's sin because he has been called to carry their burden as his own even though he did not cause the burden. He feels responsible for the people under his care.[7]

When Daniel described Israel and Judah's sin, he used multiple terms like "sinned, done wrong, acted wickedly, rebelled" (v. 5). Daniel became a prosecuting attorney and built an irrefutable case against the people. He acknowledged that their exile was just and right. Why? Because "the LORD our God is righteous in all He has done" (v. 14). Israel's public shame was deserved because it had disrespected "the great and awe-inspiring God who keeps his gracious covenant" (v. 4). Therefore, "the promised curse written in the law of Moses, the servant of God, has been poured out on us" (v. 11; see Lev. 26:14-43; Deut. 28:15-68).

Amazingly, this portion of the prayer (Dan. 9:4-14) ends with the indictment "But we have not obeyed [the Lord]" (v. 14). Dale Davis explains:

> Daniel seems to be saying that though Israel has gone through the ravages of God's curse, the people remained unchanged, unbroken, unrepentant. ... Israel has a history of rebellion and idolatry and has suffered God's judgment for it but it has not driven them to godly grief and genuine repentance. ... What good will it do to have a people back in the land with still no sense of their sin and no exercise in repentance? Who have never been crushed in spirit over their idolatry? It's not Israel alone—humanity in general is averse to admitting sin and guilt.[8]

To such an accusation we all must confess, "Guilty as charged."

PRAYER

Enter this time with your Bible and your heart open.
Based on the truths of Scripture, answer the following
questions and let them lead you to a time of prayer.

PRAISE

A large portion of Daniel's prayer consists of confession of sin. Why should
you praise God because you're able to confess your sins to Him?

REPENT

What sins do you need to confess to God today? Are there some things in the
past for which you've refused to take responsibility that you need to confess?

APPLY

God's Word leads you to know where you've sinned. What passages of
Scripture can you use this week to help you pray prayers of confession?

YIELD

Daniel said God had compassion and forgiveness even though Israel had
sinned. Do you believe God will be compassionate and forgiving if you repent
of your sin?

In light of Scripture and based on your responses,
quiet yourself before the Lord and spend a few moments in prayer.

PETITIONS AND PLEAS GROUNDED IN GOD'S CHARACTER

Read Daniel 9:15-19.

Before the righteous Judge (God) and the prosecuting attorney (Daniel), God's people had been tried and found guilty. There would be no retrial. The evidence was too great. Was there than any hope? Mercifully, the answer was yes. Sinclair Ferguson offers helpful insight about this passage:

> Daniel sees the righteousness of God both as the basis for God's judgment of the people (v. 7) and also the basis for his own prayer for forgiveness (v. 16). How can this be? In Scripture, "righteousness" basically means "integrity." Sometimes it is defined as "conformity to a norm." In the case of God the norm to which He conforms is His own being and character. He is true to Himself; He always acts in character.[9]

In a prayer that was God-centered but people-oriented,[10] Daniel appealed to "the great and awe-inspiring God who keeps His gracious covenant" (v. 4) to act for the sake of His own name, to move according to His character, righteousness, and "abundant compassion" (v. 18). In verse 15 Daniel appealed to the exodus and to God's gracious deliverance of a sinful, undeserving people. In verse 16 he appealed to God's righteous acts and pled that the Lord would turn away His "anger and wrath" from "your city Jerusalem." Why? Because "Jerusalem and your people have become an object of ridicule to all those around us" (v. 16). Dale Davis is right in saying, "Daniel batters heaven with appeals to God's honour."[11] Daniel acknowledged that the city, the hill, the people, and the sanctuary all belonged to God. Daniel's focus was on God.

Daniel's plea began to build as he asked God to "hear the prayer and the petitions of your servant" (v. 17). Then, reaching a crescendo, he cried , "Lord, hear! Lord, forgive! Lord, listen and act!" (v. 19). In effect, Daniel was saying, "Don't do it for our sake, for we're undeserving. Do it because it will bring glory to Your name and show the nations who You are and what You're like. Restore Your name and reputation for Your sake. We aren't worthy, but Lord, you are!"

PRAYER

*Enter this time with your Bible and your heart open.
Based on the truths of Scripture, answer the following
questions and let them lead you to a time of prayer.*

PRAISE

Daniel could pray to God for mercy because he knew God was dedicated
to His people. Praise God that He has linked Himself with His followers.
He will not abandon them.

REPENT

Daniel's motivation to ask for forgiveness was God's name. How often do
you pray for forgiveness because you fear the consequences or have ulterior
motives? What should be your motivation to pray?

APPLY

How can you change your prayer today to focus more on God than yourself?
What characteristics about God can you appeal to as you pray?

YIELD

Daniel was confident that God would forgive Israel and would be merciful.
Are you confident that when you pray, God will hear and answer?

*In light of Scripture and based on your responses,
quiet yourself before the Lord and spend a few moments in prayer.*

RESTING IN THE WORK OF CHRIST

Read Hebrews 7:22–25.

The Bible teaches us that prayer can accomplish great works, especially when a man of God intercedes for the people of God. In Exodus 32 Moses pled with God not to destroy the people for their idolatry. Instead, he asked God to take his life in their place. In response to Moses' prayer, God didn't annihilate Israel (see vv. 31-35). Similarly, Daniel also identified himself with his people, making their sin his sin. We don't know whether the rest of Israel was praying to God, but we know Daniel was interceding for his people. Both Daniel and Moses anticipated Jesus, the greater Moses and the greater Daniel who would identify Himself with those He would save and substitute Himself in death, taking their place and bearing the punishment for their sin.

Prayer plays an important role in the past and in the present. In the past our Lord was troubled and wept in prayer in the garden of Gethsemane as He prepared to take on the sins of the world and the wrath of God. But in the present, as Romans 8:34 and Hebrews 7:25 tell us, we have an intercessor in heaven, a great High Priest. The job of the high priest was to represent Israel before God. Now Jesus is our High Priest, who intercedes for us like no other. He pleads our cause before "the great and awesome God" (Dan. 9:4, ESV).

The prayer of Moses should elicit our admiration. The prayer of Daniel should inspire our emulation. The prayer of Jesus should move us to adoration. His prayers led Him to experience "public shame" (Dan. 9:7) in our place. His prayers led our God to forgive. Hearing the prayers of His own dear Son, our God paid attention and acted, raising Jesus from the dead, who then ascended on high, where He's "able to save completely those who come to God through him, since he always lives to intercede for them" (Heb. 7:25). Recognizing all Jesus has done for us should move our hearts to praise and adoration.

PRAYER

Enter this time with your Bible and your heart open.
Based on the truths of Scripture, answer the following
questions and let them lead you to a time of prayer.

PRAISE

Jesus is the greatest answer to the greatest prayer you could ever pray.
Praise Jesus that He gave Himself so that you could have eternal life and
true forgiveness of your sins.

REPENT

Have you asked Jesus to substitute Himself for your sins? Are you trusting
Him and not your goodness as the only source of your salvation?

APPLY

If you've trusted in Jesus, He has forgiven your past and secured your future.
How does this truth allow you to live differently in the present?

YIELD

What does it change about your prayers to know that Jesus intercedes
with God the Father on your behalf?

In light of Scripture and based on your responses,
quiet yourself before the Lord and spend a few moments in prayer.

The
Prayer
of
Nehemiah

Welcome to group session 12 of *Praying at the Crossroads.*

Use the following questions to begin the session.

Do you view your current life context as a special place of ministry? Why or why not?

Our Old Testament leader for this lesson is Nehemiah, a servant placed in a strategic position of service to the King of Persia.

How often do you sense that your activities, plans, and prayers matter to the Lord? Explain.

Nehemiah had a profound awareness of the importance of his relationship to God and the significance of his decisions.

Before we start exploring Nehemiah's powerful prayer, let's get a wide-angle view of his context. The Jewish people were living in captivity under the authority of the Persian Empire. The final generations that had survived the exile were in the area of modern-day Iran and Iraq. Some of these Jewish captives had risen to significant positions of leadership, despite coming from a different race from the leaders of the empire. (Daniel and Esther are well-known examples.) God was truly at work as He fulfilled His promise both to discipline and to restore His children.

The first two waves of thousands of Jewish exiles had returned to Israel, as chronicled in the Book of Ezra. The Lord was reestablishing His presence in the Holy Land by leading His people to rebuild the temple, study His Word, and turn their hearts back to Him in worship.

These events preceded our current text in the Book of Nehemiah. In the course of examining this week's prayer, we'll see that Nehemiah had his share of turmoil and uncertainty, but God was at work fulfilling His covenant promises.

Use these statements to follow along as you watch video session 12.

Nehemiah was a planner, a manager, and an administrator.

Nehemiah would fulfill his responsibilities faithfully to Artaxerxes, but ultimately, he was a follower of Yahweh, the King of Zion.

Zerubbabel and Ezra led the first two waves of exiles returning to Jerusalem. Nehemiah would be called upon to lead the third.

Nehemiah was standing at his crossroads of crisis.

In Nehemiah we get a glimpse into the heart of a godly leader.

Alternatives to Fight or Flight
1. Paralysis
2. Prayer

Three Aspects of Prayer and Waiting
1. The vision matures in us.
2. We mature in preparation for the vision.
3. God is at work behind the scenes.

Nehemiah's Prayer
- Nehemiah addressed the Lord and described His power and character (v. 5).
- Nehemiah made an appeal for a hearing before God's throne (v. 6).
- Nehemiah voiced a powerful, moving confession and prayed for grace for himself, his family, and his nation (vv. 6-7).
- Nehemiah rehearsed God's covenant promises, believing the Lord would draw His people back to Zion (vv. 8-9).
- Nehemiah presented a request for the people and his own personal situation (vv. 10-11).

With God's help and a godly vision, Nehemiah inspired people to join hands with him to rebuild the wall.

Step in the shoes of Nehemiah and stand with him at his crossroads of crisis.

Video sessions available at lifeway.com/prayingatthecrossroads or with a subscription to smallgroup.com

DISCUSS

Use the following questions to discuss the video teaching.

Read Nehemiah 1.

When have you seen God do something so incredible that only He could take the credit for it?

Nehemiah is an incredible and unexpected story. Through these thirteen chapters God moved a third wave of his people back to inhabit Jerusalem. The residents of the city rallied together to rebuild the city's walls in just fifty-two days. Nehemiah successfully overcame hostile opposition. In the end the city worshiped together to recognize all God had done.

At the center of this story is one incredible man—Nehemiah. He started out as a cupbearer to the king but eventually became a construction foreman, governor, worship leader, and spiritual leader. These events provide a backdrop for Nehemiah's prayer in chapter 1. We meet Nehemiah before all the success, and when we meet him, the situation is dire.

What was happening in Jerusalem at the beginning of the Book of Nehemiah? Why were these occurrences significant?

How did Nehemiah respond to the news? What does his response tell us about Nehemiah?

Above all else, Nehemiah was a devout man of prayer. When we meet Nehemiah, he had just received a letter informing him that the walls surrounding Jerusalem were broken down. While other people were content to let the walls of Jerusalem lie in disrepair, Nehemiah was grieved to his core. In his distress He called out to the God of heaven. God heard Nehemiah's prayer and answered him.

Looking at Nehemiah's résumé, we must ask several questions about the way God prepared this man to lead in such complex, diverse activities.

Where did Nehemiah learn how to request the right resources for his trip?

How did Nehemiah gain knowledge about construction materials and the engineering skill needed for this particular project? How did his unique experience in the court of the king prepare him for what God was calling Him to?

Nehemiah gained this knowledge while serving in the throne room of the most powerful leader in the world. God's plan, however, also required spiritual and intellectual preparation.

Nehemiah responded to the situation in Jerusalem with brokenness, determined to seek the Lord, and expectantly waited for His response.

What does Nehemiah's prayer in chapter 1 teach us about the type of man he was?

How was Nehemiah's character connected to the way God used him?

What qualities have you identified in yourself that make you responsive to difficult moments of crisis? What are your instinctive reactions?

Each of us has skills and talents that are useful in a time of crisis. Perhaps you have a positive, can-do attitude; are a bright, logical thinker; are a team builder who rallies others; or are spiritually sensitive to God's leading. We can learn from Nehemiah that when God calls on us to lead, He will use our abilities and gifts and will equip us to fulfill His purpose.

What qualities do you have that might discourage you from going to the Lord in prayer?

No matter what our natural talents are, we all must lean on the Lord. Often we treat prayer as a last resort. I hope this study has convinced you that prayer is our first line of defense, just as it was for Nehemiah.

GROUP PRAYER

Use the following PRAY framework to pray together as a group.

In light of what we've studied today, pray together as a group, using the following prompts to guide your experience together. You'll repeat this exercise at the end of each day's personal study. Use the biblical prayer we studied to guide your own. Read each prompt aloud and encourage group members to lift up prayers based on these prompts silently or aloud, depending on their comfort level.

PRAISE *God for who He is and what He has done.*
As Nehemiah did, speak to the Lord using His names found in Scripture, along with qualities you've found to be true about your Creator.

REPENT *of unconfessed sins and accept Christ's forgiveness.*
Nehemiah recognized the national and personal sins that brought about God's discipline in the form of the exile. Confess the ways we've sinned individually and collectively.

APPLY *the truths you've learned by committing to action.*
Remember and repeat the promises of God throughout Scripture that reveal His loving-kindness for us and that ultimately bring glory to Him.

YIELD *your life to God's will and kind providence.*
At the end of his prayer, Nehemiah asked for God's assistance in his struggle. Make your requests known to God as you submit to His will and plan for your life.

Close by praying for specific requests that arose during the session.

RESPOND IN PRAYER

Read Nehemiah 1:1-4.

Before we dive into Nehemiah's prayer in verses 5-11, let's get to know this exceptional leader. Nehemiah was in a prominent position of responsibility and status as the cupbearer to the king of Persia. We have no reason to think he was restless to leave or desired a job change. But in a matter of moments, he was shaken by the news from Jerusalem, and his life took on new meaning and a new vocation. H. G. M. Williamson describes Nehemiah this way:

> Nehemiah first answers his vocation not with action, but, as is right, with prayer–and prayer lasting some four months at that! This period of waiting upon God is not to be regarded as a sign of weakness on his part. From the later narrative we know that he was a dynamic man of action. But if a true vocation has been received to serve God, such a testing time of waiting is often to be expected; prayer during such a period will be an indication of whether the call has been genuine and whether commitment to it is unwavering.[1]

But Nehemiah's prayers didn't end in chapter 1. The entire story reveals a lifestyle of prayer:

- He prayed for the correct words to say to the king (see 2:4).
- He prayed for God to take action against the people who discouraged the work of rebuilding (see 4:4).
- He prayed for God's protection (see 4:9).
- He prayed that God would remember his faithfulness to the people (see 5:19).
- He offered quick prayers for strength and protection from his enemies (see 6:9,14).
- He expressed brief prayers requesting that his efforts on God's behalf would be remembered (see 13:14,22,31).

We see a wide spectrum of prayer topics—guidance, protection, strength—not just for himself but also for his coworkers who were reconstructing the wall. Nehemiah voiced these prayers to the Lord in the chaos of life. Can you maintain a heavenly focus in the midst of the traffic jams of your life?

PRAYER

Enter this time with your Bible and your heart open.
Based on the truths of Scripture, answer the following
questions and let them lead you to a time of prayer.

PRAISE

Do you consistently speak with the Lord in brief conversations of praise throughout the day, no matter what the situation is? During an extended period when you're waiting for God to act, are your moments of praise diminished? Does waiting sap your joy?

REPENT

Does unconfessed sin block your daily conversations with the Lord? Do you listen for the Holy Spirit's correction as you interact with others?

APPLY

Have you ever thought to have a conversation with God in the midst of a high-pressure situation, as Nehemiah did during his confrontation with the king? You know the Holy Spirit is present. Why not include Him in ever meeting? What upcoming conversations in your life come to mind?

YIELD

Are you at an important crossroads? Have you pulled over, out of traffic, to talk to God? Like Nehemiah, have you yielded thoughts of revenge, fears of attacks, or apprehension about the response of a powerful boss?

In light of Scripture and based on your responses,
quiet yourself before the Lord and spend a few moments in prayer.

ACKNOWLEDGE YOUR HOLY GOD

Read Nehemiah 1:5.

In verse 5 Nehemiah modeled for us a vital concept in beginning our conversations with God: turn your thoughts and perspective heavenward. He fixed his spiritual compass on what's permanent and absolute. Approaching prayer this way adjusts our gaze on the One who's immovable and eternal. Our prayer should begin in His throne room rather than focus on our challenging circumstance.

Does Nehemiah's opening sound familiar? Listen to these other voices:

> Ah, Lord—the great and awe-inspiring God who keeps His gracious covenant with those who love him and keep His commands ...
> **DANIEL 9:4**

> Our Father in heaven,
> your name be honored as holy.
> **MATTHEW 6:9**

One scholar describes Nehemiah's opening words this way:

> It deliberately postpones the cry for help, which could otherwise be faithless and self-pitying. It mounts immediately to heaven (as the Lord's prayer does), where the perspective will be right, and it reflects on the character of God.[2]

Nehemiah went on to humbly request God's attention once again on matters concerning God's children.

Begin a list of the names of God. Here's a partial list to get you started.[3]

Abba	*Father*	*Mark 14:36; Romans 8:15*
Alpha-Omega	*Beginning and End*	*Revelation 1:8*
El Shaddai	*God Almighty*	*Psalm 91:1*
Elohim	*Creator*	*Genesis 1:1*

Allow these names of the Lord to lead you into a time of prayer.

PRAYER

Enter this time with your Bible and your heart open.
Based on the truths of Scripture, answer the following
questions and let them lead you to a time of prayer.

PRAISE

What comes first—your praise and thanksgiving or your list of needs?
Be honest as you reflect this week on your perspective about who God
is and what your focus really is: knowing the God of heaven or speaking
to a divine butler you call on when you need something.

REPENT

Examine your heart and actions and confess any ways you've lowered God
to your level, failing to treat Him with the respect and awe-inspiring worship
He deserves.

APPLY

Continue working on your list of the names of God and His qualities. As you
pray today and this week, insert His names into your conversation with Him.

YIELD

Who comes first in your prayers—the Lord or yourself? Ask the Holy Spirit
to help you develop new spiritual disciplines that will positively influence
your prayer life.

In light of Scripture and based on your responses,
quiet yourself before the Lord and spend a few moments in prayer.

REALIZE YOUR NEED FOR CONFESSION

> **Read Nehemiah 1:6-7.**

We have much to learn from Nehemiah's spiritual discipline. First he reflected on God's character and His qualities that inspire our wonder and worship. This focus then led Nehemiah to reflect on his own sinfulness and separation from this great God.

Perhaps Nehemiah's corporate or communal thinking about the influence of an individual's sin on the whole is odd to you. His culture, in contrast to the emphasis on the individual in our day, placed a higher value on the shared responsibility each person has with his community. J. G. McConville explains Nehemiah's valuing of community and the individual's role this way:

> There is no blame-shifting here. When Nehemiah muses on the imperfection of the people of God, he is driven to reflect upon his own. His own sinfulness is a part of that broad canvas of wrong which accounts for all the displeasure of God which his people has known.[4]

Notice the way Ezra, a contemporary of Nehemiah and his predecessor in leadership in Jerusalem, expressed this same regret:

> My God, I am ashamed and embarrassed to lift my face toward you, my God, because our iniquities are higher than our heads and our guilt is as high as the heavens. Our guilt has been terrible from the days of our fathers until the present. Because of our iniquities we have been handed over, along with our kings and priests, to the surrounding kings, and to the sword, captivity, plundering, and open shame, as it is today.
> **EZRA 9:6-7**

Do we, like Nehemiah and Ezra, grasp the implications of our sin and the resulting separation and consequences for the individual and for the body of Christ?

PRAYER

Enter this time with your Bible and your heart open.
Based on the truths of Scripture, answer the following
questions and let them lead you to a time of prayer.

PRAISE

Do you have a deep, abiding sense of celebration when you consider God's grace and forgiveness?

REPENT

Take a few moments to consider ways you would express your reaction to your sin and its impact on you, your family, your community, and the body of Christ. How might Nehemiah's confession shape your own?

APPLY

Dealing with sin and its consequences was a necessary step in the Lord's preparation of Nehemiah as he waited for his next huge steps. How could the Lord be preparing you through this study for your next step?

YIELD

Are you fully prepared to yield to God's plan and timing, as Nehemiah was?

In light of Scripture and based on your responses,
quiet yourself before the Lord and spend a few moments in prayer.

PRAY SCRIPTURE

> **Read Nehemiah 1:8-11.**

Today's focal passage begins with Nehemiah's request for the Lord to remember His statements to Moses in the past. By *remember* (v. 8) Nehemiah meant more than just "Please don't forget" or "Keep up with my name and needs." His intent was much deeper and richer. Nehemiah was asking the Lord to take notice and was humbly requesting to be blessed according to God's will. This blessing was based on the relationship Nehemiah enjoyed with his Heavenly Father. Nehemiah made similar requests in this book, including four examples in chapter 13.

Today's focal verses contain two important insights into Nehemiah's understanding of the character and ways of God.

1. Nehemiah revealed his knowledge of God's covenant promises that He first gave to Abraham in Genesis 12:1-3; 15; and 17 and restated to Moses in Leviticus 26. Quoting Deuteronomy 30:2-4, Nehemiah demonstrated genuine faith. He had embraced God's promise, acknowledged that God would follow through with the consequences stated in His warnings, and fully trusted that He could restore His people and His name in Jerusalem. Nehemiah realized that no boundaries, political or geographic, could stand in the way of God's fulfillment of His covenant.

2. In Nehemiah 1:10 Nehemiah stated that God had redeemed the people once and believed He could do it again. Our English word *redeem* comes from a Latin word meaning "to buy back, to free from captivity by payment of ransom."[5] The Lord brought the nation out of slavery in Egypt in the past, and Nehemiah believed it was time for the Jews in exile to return to the promised land.

The return had already begun but had lost traction, and the temple lacked a protective wall. Nehemiah expressed a prayer that was based on God's promises and His past actions on behalf of His people. How soon would God rescue His children again?

Generations later the Lord would once again fulfill His promise to His children of all races in the person of His Son, the Lord Jesus. His ultimate act of redemption for all humankind would take place in the city of Jerusalem, over which Nehemiah had agonized in prayer that day.

PRAYER

Enter this time with your Bible and your heart open.
Based on the truths of Scripture, answer the following
questions and let them lead you to a time of prayer.

PRAISE

Begin your prayer time by recalling and reciting promises from Scripture. List specific promises voiced by Jesus and recorded in the Gospels. Rejoice that you serve a Savior who's worthy of your trust.

REPENT

Reflect on your walk with the Lord and evaluate your active trust in Him. What aspects of your life reveal a lack of trust?

APPLY

What changes do you need to make as you move forward? What's holding you back from walking and leading by faith?

YIELD

What are you clinging to instead of holding on to your Savior? Ask the Holy Spirit for guidance and wisdom to turn away from these idols and to turn to Jesus.

In light of Scripture and based on your responses,
quiet yourself before the Lord and spend a few moments in prayer.

MAKE YOUR REQUEST

Reread Nehemiah 1.

Perhaps you've been wondering this week, *Would I have been content to pray in Nehemiah's situation?* Chuck Swindoll lists four reasons to place a high priority on prayer:

1. Prayer makes you wait.
2. Prayer clears your vision.
3. Prayer quiets your heart.
4. Prayer activates your faith.[6]

We can see evidence of these benefits in our previous studies. Verse 11 suggests that Nehemiah was sensing it was time to act:

> Give your servant success today, and grant
> him compassion in the presence of this man.
> **NEHEMIAH 1:11**

As any of us might, Nehemiah was requesting the Lord's guidance and intervention as he prepared for a meeting with his boss. But in contrast to our situation, King Artaxerxes had the power to put Nehemiah to death if he chose.

Proverbs 21:1 gives us another biblical insight into Nehemiah's situation:

> A king's heart is like channeled water in the LORD's hand:
> He directs it wherever he chooses.
> **PROVERBS 21:1**

Consistent with the wisdom of Solomon, Nehemiah acknowledged his earthly subordination to the Persian king, but he prayed in faith that the Lord of the universe would superintend his meeting at this important intersection in his life.

204

PRAYER

Enter this time with your Bible and your heart open.
Based on the truths of Scripture, answer the following
questions and let them lead you to a time of prayer.

Let's conclude our study together by pondering our Savior's actions the night before His crucifixion. Jesus knelt in prayer at the most significant crossroads in history—the final moments before He would carry His cross to Calvary. Yielding Himself to the will of the Father, He prayed for you and me.

PRAISE

Review Jesus' prayer in John 17. Spend time celebrating your right standing with your Heavenly Father because of the sacrifice of His Son. Reflect on His selfless love in praying for future disciples during the hours before His death.

REPENT

Jesus prayed in John 17:4, "I have glorified You on the earth by completing the work you gave me to do." Take this occasion to repent of thoughts and actions that don't bring glory to the Lord.

APPLY

Nehemiah was a strong model of humility and servanthood. Jesus is the ultimate model of sacrifice for others, even submitting to death on a cruel cross. How is He calling you to lead and serve for His glory?

YIELD

Prayerfully consider anything in your life that stands in the way of your total commitment to Christ.

In light of Scripture and based on your responses,
quiet yourself before the Lord and spend a few moments in prayer.

Week 1

1. Although the psalm's heading says that Moses wrote the prayer, some claim the psalm was written by a later author. John Goldingay, in *Psalms 90–103*, vol. 3, Psalms (Grand Rapids, MI: Baker, 2008), 24, contends that "the psalm might have been written to indicate how Moses might pray for the people in their present circumstances, in light of the material in Exod. 32 and Deut. 32–33. … Here the people's situation in a time later than Moses's (e.g., after the exile) is reckoned to be similar to their situation in Moses's time." Allen P. Ross, in *A Commentary on the Psalms*, vol. 3 (90–150) (Grand Rapids, MI: Kregel, 2015), 26, however, rightly argues that none of the arguments against Mosaic authorship are "convincing." Ross notes that Moses is the appropriate choice to be the author of Psalm 90 (ibid.). He argues, "The psalm is the reflection of an old man on the passing of life; the man does not argue, nor seek vengeance on the wicked who have inflicted the pain. The wicked are the Israelites who brought the affliction on themselves because of sin. When Moses was 70 or 80, he knew the inevitable. He would die. He knows that he nor the Israelites with him who rebelled in the wilderness would see a successful end to their wandering. They are swept away in God's fury. … So the petition is for the successive generations."

2. Tremper Longmann III, *Psalms*, Tyndale Old Testament Commentaries (Downers Grove, IL: InterVarsity, 2014), 328.

3. Ross, *Psalms*, 30.

4. Nancy DeClaissé-Walford, Rolf A. Jacobson, and Beth Laneel Tanner, *The Book of Psalms*, The New International Commentary on the Old Testament (Grand Rapids, MI: Eerdmans, 2014), 694.

5. Ross, *Psalms*, 31.

6. Ibid.

7. Ibid., 32.

8. Ibid., 37.

9. Ibid., 39.

Week 6

1. Portions of this week's material were adapted from J. Chris Schofield, *Impact Prayer Guide* (Cary, NC: Baptist State Convention of North Carolina, 2017). To download this thirty-day devotional and prayer guide, visit PrayNC.org.

2. Robert Coleman, *Dry Bones Can Live Again: A Study Manual on Revival in the Local Church* (Old Tappan, NJ: Fleming H. Revell, 1969), 7.

3. For more on Zinzendorf, the Herrnhut church, and the one-hundred-year prayer movement, see Mendell L. Taylor, *Exploring Evangelism* (Kansas City, MO: Beacon Hill, 1964), 237–39, and Leslie K. Tarr, "A Prayer Meeting That Lasted One Hundred Years," *Christian History* 1, no. 1 (1982), https://christianhistoryinstitute.org/magazine/article/one-hundred-year-prayer-meeting.

Week 8

1. Israel became a divided kingdom after the reign of Solomon because of its unrelenting unfaithfulness to Yahweh (see 1 Kings 11:9-11; 12:1-24). The Northern Kingdom, made up of ten tribes, had only wicked kings and was marked primarily by wicked deeds. The Southern Kingdom, made up of two tribes, Judah and Benjamin, only sometimes walked in obedience to the Lord. Hezekiah's reign is one of those times.

2. Simon Anglim et al., *Fighting Techniques of the Ancient World*, 3000 BC–AD 500 (New York: Thomas Dunne, 2002), 12.

3. Martin Luther, "A Mighty Fortress Is Our God," *Baptist Hymnal* (Nashville: LifeWay Worship, 2008), 656.

4. F. B. Meyer, as quoted in Jerry Sittser, *When God Doesn't Answer Your Prayer* (Grand Rapids, MI: Zondervan, 2007).

5. Jim Elliot, as quoted in Hayley and Michael DiMarco, *Die Young: Burying Yourself in Christ* (Wheaton, IL: Crossway, 2012), 137.

Week 10

1. Warren W, Wiersbe, *The Prophets: Isaiah–Malachi,* The Bible Exposition Commentary, Old Testament (Colorado Springs: David C Cook, 2002), 388.

Week 11

1. John Owen, as quoted in Sinclair B. Ferguson, *Daniel,* vol. 21, The Preacher's Commentary (Nashville: Thomas Nelson, 1988), 171.
2. C. H. Spurgeon, *C. H. Spurgeon's Sermons on the Book of Daniel,* ed. Charles Thomas Cook (Grand Rapids, MI, Zondervan, 1966), 99–100.
3. This week's content borrows heavily from Daniel L. Akin, *Exalting Jesus in Daniel,* Christ-Centered Exposition (Nashville: Holman, 2017).
4. Robert S. Fyall, *Daniel: A Tale of Two Cities* (Fearn, Ross-Shire, UK: Christian Focus, 1988), 132.
5. Ibid., 147.
6. David Helm, *Daniel for You* (Epsom, UK: The Good Book Company, 2015), 159.
7. Bryan Chapell, *The Gospel According to Daniel: A Christ-Centered Approach* (Grand Rapids, MI.: Baker Books, 2014), 158.
8. Dale Ralph Davis, *The Message of Daniel,* The Bible Speaks Today (Downers Grove, IL: InterVarsity Press, 2013), 118.
9. Sinclair B. Ferguson, *Daniel,* vol. 21, The Preacher's Commentary (Nashville: Thomas Nelson, 1988), 178.
10. Ibid., 179.
11. Davis, *The Message of Daniel,* 120.

Week 12

1. H. G. M. Williamson, *Ezra-Nehemiah,* vol. 16, Word Biblical Commentary (Nashville: Thomas Nelson, 1985), 175.
2. F. D. Kidner, ibid., 172.
3. For a complete list, visit https://www.lwf.org/discover-jesus/names-of-god.
4. J. G. McConville, *Ezra, Nehemiah, and Esther,* The Daily Study Bible Series (Louisville: Westminster John Knox, 1985), 76.
5. Merriam-Webster.com, accessed November 5, 2018, https://www.merriam-webster.com/dictionary/redeem.
6. Charles R. Swindoll, *Nehemiah, Hand Me Another Brick,* rev. ed. (Nashville: Word, 1998), 41.

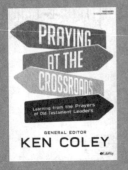

WHERE TO GO FROM HERE

We hope you enjoyed *Praying at the Crossroads*. Now that you've completed this study, here are three possible directions you can go in next.

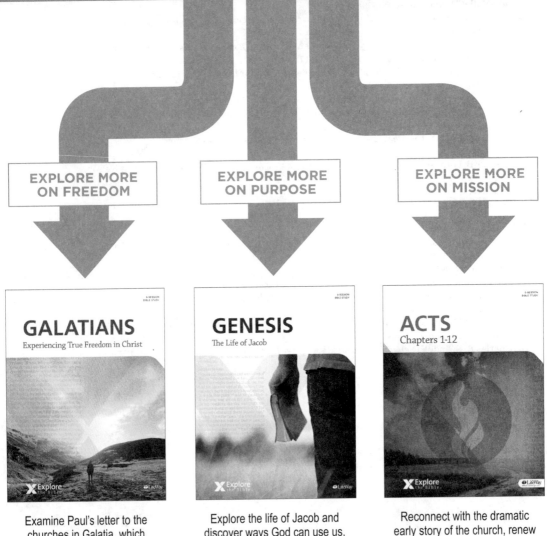

EXPLORE MORE ON FREEDOM

EXPLORE MORE ON PURPOSE

EXPLORE MORE ON MISSION

GALATIANS
Experiencing True Freedom in Christ

GENESIS
The Life of Jacob

ACTS
Chapters 1-12

Examine Paul's letter to the churches in Galatia, which exposes the fallacy of the gospel of grace-plus-law and provides solid biblical evidence for salvation by grace alone. (6 sessions)

Explore the life of Jacob and discover ways God can use us, like Jacob, to accomplish His purpose in the world in spite of our sinfulness. (6 sessions)

Reconnect with the dramatic early story of the church, renew your passion to obey the Lord, and refocus your vision as His global witness. (6 sessions)